LEADERSHIP BEGINS WITH YOU

Being a Self-Aware and Skillful Leader

CARL WELTE

Copyright © 2023 Carl Welte.

All rights reserved. No part of this book may be reproduced, stored, or transmitted by any means—whether auditory, graphic, mechanical, or electronic—without written permission of both publisher and author, except in the case of brief excerpts used in critical articles and reviews. Unauthorized reproduction of any part of this work is illegal and is punishable by law.

ISBN: 979-8-89031-628-8 (sc)
ISBN: 979-8-89031-629-5 (hc)
ISBN: 979-8-89031-630-1 (e)

Because of the dynamic nature of the Internet, any web addresses or links contained in this book may have changed since publication and may no longer be valid. The views expressed in this work are solely those of the author and do not necessarily reflect the views of the publisher, and the publisher hereby disclaims any responsibility for them.

One Galleria Blvd., Suite 1900, Metairie, LA 70001
(504) 702-6708

ALSO BY CARL WELTE

Making and Fulfilling Your Dreams as a Leader:
A Practical Guide for Formulating and Executing Strategy

Building Commitment:
Unleashing the Human Potential at Work

To all those leaders and aspiring leaders who are striving to make a difference and having a positive influence in doing so for the common good.

BEING A SELF-AWARE AND SKILLFUL LEADER

CONTENTS

Introduction ix

I. Being a *Self-Aware* Leader

1. Surfacing the Inner You: The Natural and Nurtured You 3
2. Identifying and Capitalizing on Your Strengths:
   Making the Best of Who You Are..13

II. Being a *Skillful* Self-Aware Leader

3. The Communication Process: Understanding the Basics ...35
4. Sharpening Your Perceptive Skills:
   The Map Is Not the Territory...47
5. The Structure of Magic:
   Skillfully Communicating about Differences....................69
6. Using Natural and Adaptive Behaviors:
   Aligning Your Behavior with the Situation,
   Environment, and Relationship 99

III. Self-Coaching

7. Self-Coaching: Making Personal Behavioral Change 111

Appendix A: Perception and Communication:
   Answers and Comments... 119
Endnotes 129
About the Author 135

INTRODUCTION

Being a successful leader needs to start with you as the leader. To deal with uncertainty, ride the unpredictable waves, and effectively address the countless opportunities and challenges that come with being a leader, you need to continually engage in quality thinking and interacting to move things to new and better places. And the more you are in touch with just who you are and what you stand for, the more prepared you will be to be an authentic and skillful leader. That is what this book is about.

I believe there are three imperatives for being a successful leader.

- Being a Self-Aware and Skillful Leader
- Formulating and Executing a Sound Strategy
- Building a Culture of Commitment

My book *Making and Fulfilling Your Dreams as a Leader: A Practical Guide for Formulating and Executing Strategy* equips you as the leader to architect and live a *Sound Strategy* for the organization as a whole or your organizational entity.

My book *Building Commitment: A Leader's Guide to Unleashing the Human Potential at Work* equips the leader to effectively use the four requisite building blocks—Selection, Clarity, Performance Coaching, and Growing Teams—to *Build a Culture of Commitment* allowing people to be excited about achieving the sound strategy.

Part I of the book, helps you discover and appreciate the real you. Chapter One, *Surfacing the Inner You*, allows you to get in touch with your subconscious tendencies, priorities, and preferences. Doing so allows you to be more self-aware of both the natural and nurtured you. The value is that you are in a much better position to understand your thoughts, feelings, and behavior and to benefit accordingly.

Chapter Two, *Identifying and Capitalizing on Your Strengths*, allows you to do just that. You are just more productive and happier when you position yourself to do things you are good at and passionate about.

Part II of the book discusses three critical interactive competencies needed for you to be a *skillful* self-aware leader. These three critical skill sets are:

- **Being Perceptive:** Understanding and appreciating just what is going on.
- **Communicating about Differences:** Effectively using listening and speaking communication patterns to seek to understand and be understood.
- **Being Behaviorally Flexible:** To use both natural and adaptive behaviors to align with the situation, environment, and relationships you are dealing with.

Chapter Three, *The Communication Process: Understanding the Basics*, lays the groundwork for the ensuing chapters in this section. It lays out the basic elements of the communication process. But it does more than that by discussing some aspects of communication that you may not realize, and that can be very valuable to you.

Chapter Four, *Sharpening Your Perceptive Skills: The Map Is Not the Territory*, helps you assess the current situation so you can respond appropriately. Chapter Five, *The Structure of Magic: Skillfully Communicating about Differences*, discusses effective communication patterns to sharpen your listening and speaking skills allowing you to have constructive conversations, especially when communicating about divergent points of view. Chapter Six, *Using Natural and Adaptive*

Behaviors: Aligning Your Behavior with the Situation, Environment, and Relationship, helps you understand the importance and value of using both natural and adaptive behaviors to best align with what is called for.

Part III is comprised of Chapter Seven, *Self-Coaching: Making Personal Improvements*. It serves well as the final chapter of the book. You are provided a comprehensive, practical, and proven process for engaging in quality thinking, planning, and acting to make any personal behavioral changes you deem appropriate to optimize some of the insights gained from the book.

I trust that you will find this book to be an invaluable resource for you as you continue to grow as a leader.

I

BEING A *SELF-AWARE* LEADER

This section of the book guides you to go to a deeper level than you have probably ever experienced before to surface your subconscious natural and nurtured tendencies, priorities, and preferences. This higher level of self-awareness enables you to better understand just what is driving a lot of your thinking and feeling, allowing you to make more informed decisions on how to think and act in the moment. It also allows you to assess self-improvement efforts you may want to make and how to go about it.

This section also enables you to identify and capitalize on your strengths. Your strengths are the things you are good at and passionate about. This awareness allows you to make better decisions about just how you want to live your life and spend your time. Who does not want to focus on things they are good at and like to do?

1

SURFACING THE INNER YOU: THE NATURAL AND NURTURED YOU

"You are a product of the of the practices you engage in (your behavior), and the current mental models you carry around (your thinking).

—Carl Welte

Level of Consciousness: The degree to which one is aware of self and others, and uses such awareness to enhance communications and relationships.

—Carl Welte

The Value of Knowing the Real You

The Value for Anyone

Significant value comes from a heightened level of self-awareness. Being aware of the key drivers of your thoughts, feelings, and behavior allows you to better manage yourself.

Some of the specific benefits derived from a heightened level of awareness are that you will:

- Have an easier time being authentic.

- Enhance your personal effectiveness (doing the right things) and efficiency (doing things right).

- Have greater peace of mind.

- Be better able to define and navigate your destiny.

  You are better able to create or choose paths that are right for you instead of trusting your fate to others.

  "Define your destiny, or someone else will."
  —Noel Tichy

  "Who would you be if no one ever told you who you should be?"
  —Wayne Dyer

- Be better able to glide instead of grind in performing work.

- Have greater clarity in architecting personal improvements.

The Value for Leaders

In addition to the values cited above, having greater self-awareness is especially valuable for leaders.

You as a leader will:

- Have greater confidence in choosing leadership roles for yourself.

  You are better able to assess the opportunities and challenges afforded by a specific leadership role and your personal attributes, your natural and nurtured tendencies, priorities, and preferences. In addition, you can better assess the degree to which your personal values align with those of the organization.

- Be better equipped to model the way as a leader in building the culture or climate for the organization as a whole or for your organizational entity.

As the leader you need to assure that your organization's core values are both clear and lived. You must both "Talk the Talk" and "Walk the Talk." This is called integrity.

- Have greater confidence in being authentic and honest.

  In their exhaustive research over many decades spanning the globe and including organizations from all business sectors and leaders at all organizational levels, Jim Kouzes and Barry Posner of The Leadership Challenge fame, have found that honesty is consistently ranked the number one characteristic of admired leaders.[1]

- Find it easier to be inspiring. Being inspiring is another characteristic of admired leaders that Kouzes and Posner found consistently ranks at the top.

  We are not necessarily talking about the "rah-rah" brand of inspiration here, although there is nothing wrong with being enthusiastic and demonstrating it. Jim Collins found that in his research, the most effective leaders were those who inspired others through the passion they displayed and their collaborative leadership behavior.[2]

- Have greater courage to lead.

  You are more likely to take risks and to be bold. Having greater confidence in knowing who you are enables you to know that you do not need to have all the answers. You are more willing to be collaborative in their problem-solving, decision-making, and action-planning. You are okay with being vulnerable. As Brené Brown stresses, vulnerability gives birth to courage opening the door for innovation, creativity, managing difficult conversations, and adaptability to change.[3]

- Be more consistent in your thinking and behavior.

  People have a difficult time following inconsistent leaders. It is very frustrating.

- Have greater confidence to manage the rigors of leadership.

  To be an effective leader you need to be able to ride the waves. You need to constructively deal with the ups and downs that come with leadership: the uncertainties and the surprises. You need to effectively manage divergent points of view. And to live with the fact that you are not always going to be popular. This all requires confidence that emanates from a heightened level of self-awareness.

- Surround yourself with people who "complement," not "compliment" you. You have the personal security not to require constant affirmation.

The Inner You

Most of our everyday thoughts, feelings, and actions stem from our subconscious. They are reflexive in nature, coming from the habitual you.

An iceberg is a perfect metaphor to think about the conscious and subconscious you. The part of the iceberg that is above water represents just a small fraction of the total mass. Estimates run as high as 97 percent of the iceberg is underwater. Hence the expression, "It's just the tip of the iceberg."

Figure 1.1 Relationship of the Conscious and Subconscious You

The Conscious You
(Cognitive Consciousness)

The Subconscious You
(The Reflexive, Habitual You)

Your subconscious tendencies, priorities, and preferences

THE INNER YOU

Before exploring the dimensions of the Inner You, let us look at *what you are not.*

<u>**Your False Self**</u>
(The Lies Your Ego Tells You)
Wayne Dyer[4]

1. **Who I am is not what I have.**

    You are not the materialistic things you own. Such things as houses, cars, boats, expensive hobbies, and the like. Some people take such things as symbols of success. They may spend their entire adult life chasing after them; always wanting more and striving to get something bigger and better than their neighbors.

    The problem with this mindset of evaluating ourselves based on what we have acquired is: *If we are what we have, then who are we when we no longer have such materialistic possessions?*

2. **Who I am is what I do.**

    We learn that doing things, especially if we do them better than others, is rewarding. Reinforcement for performing is not bad. But it teaches us to believe that "You are what you do," which of course is false. This type of mindset equates a person's worth with what they have accomplished.

The problem with this mindset of evaluating ourselves on accomplishments, positions held, or social status is: *If we are what we do, what we have accomplished, or our social status, then who are we when we no longer can accomplish such things, hold such positions, or have the social status we once had?*

3. **Who I am is what others think of me.**

   Throughout life, we get messages attempting to convince us that our worth comes from the observations and opinions of others. But self-esteem stems from internally held positive beliefs about ourselves, not from the approval of others. Who you are, the authentic or real you has nothing to do with the thoughts or opinions of others.

   The problem with this mindset of evaluating ourselves based on what others think of us is: *Who are you when people change their minds about you, and no longer think you are intelligent, talented, beautiful, or whatever?*

Putting this all together, the question comes down to this: *"Do you want to be the Hostage of the External Me or the Host of the Real Me?"*

Dimensions of the Inner You

There are two dimensions of the Inner You: your Core and your Mental Models.

Your Core is the Natural You. What you were born with. Your Mental Model is the Nurtured You. What you have picked up as you have lived your life.

Figure 1.2 Dimensions of the Inner You

CORE	MENTAL MODELS
The Natural You	**The Nurtured You**
Your uniqueness coming into the world. Your "hard-wiring"	• Formed by your **life experiences.** • Your **sensitivity** to such experiences. That is your *understanding* of such experiences and the *impact* they had on you.
Elements • Physical characteristics • Abilities • Talents • Traits • Temperament	**Elements** • Beliefs • Values • Assumptions

Categories of some life experiences that probably helped shape your Mental Models:

- Upbringing
- Education
- Economic situations
- Social settings
- Ideologies (e.g., religious, political, cultural)
- Work/career
- Admired people
- Teachers/coaches/mentors
- People who have cared about you
- Mental/physical well-being.

Your Mental Models can become just as "hard-wired" as your Core. Think of how brutally many humans have treated other humans throughout history. Fighting and killing over who has the right religion; lives in the right country; or belongs to the right tribe. And the hate that some people carry around based on a person's origin, looks, the color of their skin, or political beliefs.

Surfacing Your Core Drivers

There are three primary inputs to help you surface your Core:

- Self-observation and reflection of your personal experiences.
- Constructive feedback from others.
- Behavioral and psychological profile assessment instruments. Instruments such as D.I.S.C.; Myers-Briggs Type Indicator; and the Enneagram.

Figure 1.3 Inputs for Discovering Your Core

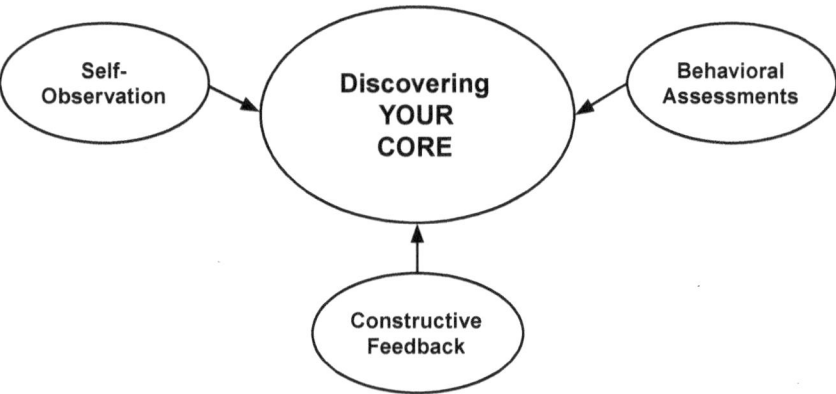

What to Do

1. Thinking of the elements of your Core (Physical Characteristics; Talents/Abilities; Temperament; Traits), reflect on what the inputs are telling you about your Core.

2. Use a word or two to describe each of your *Key* Core Drivers. *Limit to your most significant Core Drivers.*

   Some miscellaneous examples: Visionary; Loyal; Conscientious; Relationship Orientation; Tenacious; Intuitive; Action Orientation; Directive; Fact-Based; Analytical; Steadiness; Perfectionist.

As far as behavioral or psychological assessment instruments are concerned, they are not essential, but they can serve to supplement and perhaps reinforce your self-observation and constructive feedback relative to surfacing your Core Drivers. Assure that whatever assessment instrument you may be considering, assure that it is comprehensive, valid, and reliable.

Based on my extensive experience with such instruments, my recommendation is the DISC behavioral assessment instrument. It is a solid instrument with an easy to understand and apply model.

There are several purveyors of the DISC. My recommendation is Assessments 24x7.[5] The recommendation is based on a professional relationship I have had with the Assessments 24x7 organization for many years. Their products are first-rate. The assessment instrument is easy to take. You can do it online. Their feedback reports are very comprehensive and professional.

A caveat regarding the use of assessment instruments. They do not take the place of your real-world inputs, that is, your self-observation and constructive feedback. But, as mentioned earlier, they can be useful to supplement or reinforce your effort to surface your key Core Drivers.

Also, you are far too complex for any assessment instrument to capture the real inner you. Realize that the best they can do is provide some useful approximations for you to ponder.

And for heaven's sake, as far as you as a leader are concerned, if you and your team take any assessments, use the results judiciously. Do not overdo any feedback you receive. And do not pretend that you are now able to predict individual behavior. Again, people are far too complex for any instrument to be highly predictive of behavior.

Surfacing Your Mental Models

What to Do

1. Thinking of the elements of Mental Models (Beliefs; Values; Assumptions), do some quality reflection to surface your important few Mental Models that *currently* play a large role in influencing your thinking, feelings, and behavior. I use the word currently because you are strongly encouraged to adopt a *growth mindset* as contrasted with a *fixed mindset*.[6] As an aware adult, you need to continually assess your Mental Models, and as called for, update or revise them based on new realities. Many people do not do so, greatly limiting their level of consciousness, and getting mired in assumptions that do not reflect current realities.

2. Use a word or two to describe each of your current important Mental Models.

    For the sake of example, let me share mine: Family First; Be an Authentic Me; Honesty and Integrity; Optimize My Potential; Balanced Life; Respect Everyone; Be a "Giver" not a "Taker."

Having used the Dimensions of the Inner You, your Core and Mental Models, to help you better understand the real you, we now turn to another important aspect to help you understand and appreciate the real you. That is to identify your strengths. Strengths are the things you are really good at and passionate about. And then capitalize on putting your strengths to work for you.

2

IDENTIFYING AND CAPITALIZING ON YOUR STRENGTHS: MAKING THE BEST OF WHO YOU ARE

"Don't waste time trying to put in what was left out. Try to draw on what was left in. That is hard enough."

—Marcus Buckingham and Curt Coffman

In furthering our efforts to help you know the real you, we move from surfacing the Inner You (your Core and Mental Models) to helping you identify your Strengths, and then to capitalize on them.

What Are Strengths?

Strengths: Things you are really good at and passionate about.

To be considered a strength, it must be something you are *both* good at and passionate about.

There may be things that you were once good at but your capability, be it physical or mental, has waned. Or perhaps you still could excel in a certain specialty but have lost the desire you once possessed.

On the other hand, you may be very passionate about something but, in all honesty, do not possess the natural ability to excel. We often refer to these activities as hobbies.

Your strengths in essence represent the manifestation of your Inner Self. That is your Core, the Natural you and your Mental Models, the Nurtured you, springing to life.

The Difference between Ability and Skill

There is an important distinction to be made between ability and skill.

Ability has to do with your *personal capacity or potential* to perform a specific activity or task.

Skill has to do with your *current competence* to perform a specific activity or task, regardless of your personal capacity or potential.

Let us use the metaphor of the amount of liquid level in a container to help make the distinction between ability and skill.

Figure 2.1   The Difference between Ability and Skill

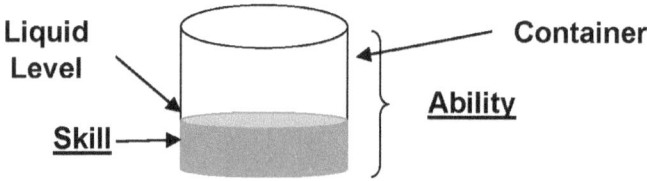

There are of course all kinds of abilities. Abilities such as mechanical, mathematical, athletic, intellectual, manual dexterity, just to name a few.

Your capability or potential (the size of your container) will of course vary from one category of ability to the next. You have greater or less ability in some areas than other areas. And there are abilities you may not even be aware of. We call these latent abilities.

Age affects abilities that require physical effort. As a young person grows and gets stronger, their potential to perform physical activities increases. On the other end, as we age our physical capabilities most often ebb. And for some, as they age, their mental capacity also shrinks.

Your skill level fluctuates, regardless of your natural potential or capability in a particular area. As you apply yourself through study, exercising, and deliberate practice your skill level should rise. By the same token, your skill level is likely to decrease if you do not, as the expression goes: "Keep your skills honed." Another common related expression: "I am a little rusty. I haven't played for a while."

The Value of Identifying Your Strengths

The benefits reaped from identifying your strengths are significant.

Knowing your strengths allows you to:

- Optimize your decision-making.
- Create or choose the best work/career options.
- "Glide" versus "grind" in performing work.
- Be more effective and efficient.
- Have more fun.

Identifying Your Strengths

A Powerful and Fun Exercise to Identify Your Strengths[1]

There are three parts to this exercise.

What to Do

PART I

Recall *three times* when you were at your leadership best.

Perhaps it was a major opportunity or challenge you took on. Or maybe it was a major project or assignment that you lead or played a major role in.

Your organizational leadership work experiences are typically your best choices for benefitting from this exercise. You may have been either the formal or informal leader. But you may also have some community, civic, or volunteer work that could also serve as good examples of when you were at your leadership best.

PART II

Use a sheet of paper to describe each of your leadership best experiences. Use the structure shown below to describe each of your leadership best experiences.

Figure 2.2 Describing a Time When I Was at My Leadership Best

My Leadership Best Experience: _____

Phase/Stage:	Memorable Thoughts/Feelings/Behavior/Achievements
Start Up *(How I was drawn in)*	
Getting Things Rolling	
Keeping Things Rolling	*Make appropriate notations for each phase of the experience*
Wrapping Things Up	

An Example

My Leadership Best Experience: Growing an Organizational Leadership Development Capability

Phase/Stage	
Start-Up	Why me? Why now? Doubts/Concerns I had.
	What to do? Who to turn to for help? Experiencing feelings of angst.
	Getting my bearings. Getting educated.
	Excitement about gaining new knowledge and skills.
	Sketching things out. Fun designing, experimenting, and collaborating.
	Developing an initial blueprint. Achievement.
Getting Things Rolling	Staffing up.
	Developing people.
	Experimentation.
	New training offerings.
	Results. Pride. Encouragement.
Keeping Things Rolling	Putting the show on the road.
	Providing consulting in addition to training. Great results.
	Growing an organization development reputation.
	Leading the effort successfully for several years.
Wrapping Things Up	Leaving things in good hands as I moved on.
	Satisfaction from a job well done.

PART III

Reflect on each of your three stories.

Weave a thread through the three stories to identify common themes. That is, things you did or were engaged in when you were at your leadership best.

1. Record the results of your reflection and analysis by using a series of *"I feel strongest when ------------------------------------"* statements.

   Example

   Let us use the analysis of the leader in the example used above after reviewing his three leadership best stories and identifying common themes.

   "I feel strongest when *presented with an opportunity or challenge which is not well defined, if at all, and I need to define success."*

   "I feel strongest when *I need to develop the blueprint and roadmap to achieve the desired results."*

   "I feel strongest when *I need to pull all the pieces together for the effort to be a success."*

   "I feel strongest when *successful genuine collaboration and teamwork needs to occur to achieve the desired results."*

   "I feel successful when *I and the members of the team experience real learning and growth."*

   "I feel strongest when *I lead an effort from architecting the desired results to crafting appropriate strategies and needed implementation actions to successfully move the effort to completion or implementation."*

   "I feel strongest when *the necessary protocols and capabilities are in place for the effort to sustain success."*

2. Convert your Strength Statements into Strength Descriptors, consisting of one to three words.

   Example

   The leader spearheaded the growing organizational development capability and identified the following Descriptors after completing the "I feel strongest when ---------------" statements.

   - Strategic Thinker
   - Systems Thinker
   - Genuine Collaborator
   - Practical Problem Solver
   - Action Orientation

An Additional Resource

Donald Clifton and Marcus Bellingham have done some good work in helping people identify their strengths. They use the term Strength Finder to refer to their work.[2]

Their current instrument is listed under *Gallup Clifton Strength Assessment*. It is comprised of 34 themes of human development.

I prefer using the three best leadership experiences described above. It provides a more visceral experience and more specific results that you identified allowing for a better understanding and ownership of your strengths. It also is a lot more fun.

Defining Your Identity

An *organization's Identity* consists of two components. The first component is the organization's Purpose. An organization's Purpose is a powerfully worded one-word sentence summarizing *"Why we exist."* The second component is Core Values, which clarify *"What we stand for."*

Although there is some variation in definition and application, the same two components can be used to define one's identity as an individual.

But rather than start with defining Purpose in defining your personal Identity, most times it works best to first get in touch with the real you, and let your Purpose flow from and summarize what you really are all about. In other words, complete first the work previously discussed to surface the Inner You (your Core and Mental Models) and identify your Strengths. And then to ask these questions: *"What does all this add up to for me?" "What is my Purpose?"*

Although your Inner You is different and broader than an organization's Core Values, it does set a natural foundation for defining your Purpose. And that is why for individual versus organizational application it makes sense to invert the sequencing of the two components

For me, after reviewing the inner me and my strengths, my Purpose was clear. I am really all about serving and supporting others, especially when it comes to helping clarify direction and making sound decisions.

Capitalizing on Your Strengths

Knowing your strengths allows you to create and choose the best options for you moving forward. But why wait? Let us go to work on your current leadership role to see if we can find ways to capitalize on your strengths.

An Exercise

There are three parts to this exercise:

> Part I Scope out your current Leadership Playing Field.
>
> Part II Mine your Leadership Playing Field to identify possible ways to capitalize on your strengths.
>
> Part III Plot appropriate implementation strategies.

We will start by having you identify your **Key Result Areas** (KRAs).

Your Key Result Areas (KRAs) represent your *major areas of accountability or responsibility*.

But first, we need to make a key distinction between accountability and responsibility.

Figure 2.3 The Distinction between Accountability and Responsibility

> **Accountability:**   The obligation to *achieve desired results*.
>
> **Responsibility:**   The obligation to *perform specific activities*.

As a leader, you can delegate responsibilities, but you cannot delegate your accountability.

Your KRAs stem from the three categories of organizational work as shown below.

Figure 2.4 The Work of the Organization

> **Technical Work:**   The direction application of physical and mental effort to achieve the work of the organization. That is, to produce its products and services.
>
> **Management Work:**   The coordination of diverse activities to achieve desired results.
>
> **Leadership:**   Mobilizing people to struggle to achieve shared aspirations.

Figure 2.5 The Distinction between Management and Leadership

Management		Leadership
The Here and Now	**Focus**	The Future
Coordination	**Essence**	Achieving a Desired Future State

Although in a general sense, it is important to understand the distinction between leadership and management, when it comes to clarifying leadership and management expectations, the distinction often gets blurred. Consequently, I recommend combining the two, as shown in the examples below, when it comes to clarifying expectations, or in our immediate application, listing KRAs.

Examples of Key Result Areas (KRAs)

General Manager, Water District

1. Leadership and Management
2. Customer Service
3. Engineering
4. Operation and Maintenance
5. Finance and Administration

VP Information Systems, Bank

1. Leadership and Management
2. Project Management
3. Account Management
4. Infrastructure Design and Maintenance
5. Application Integration

Let us talk about the rationale for including Leadership and Management as a KRA.

When you think about it, leadership and management can be thought of as overhead work. The results of performing such work are indirect.

The benefits derived from effective leadership and management work are realized through a more effective and efficient performance of the organization's technical work.

This is not to underestimate the value of leadership and management. Far from it. Such work is critical to optimize the achievement of desired results. And when well performed, such work can result in extraordinary outcomes that would not otherwise be possible.

That is why it is critical to include leadership and management as a KRA for any position that has a leadership role as part of its accountability.

Having a leadership and management KRA for any position that has a leadership/management role allows you as the leader to develop leadership and management expectations for yourself and any leader/managers reporting to you.

Given that the results of good leadership and management are achieved through improved technical results, desired leadership and management expectations are often more activity than results related. That is okay. They will get translated into results with the performance of the technical work.

Besides the critical importance of effective leadership and management to the achievement of the organization's identity and direction, there are several other important reasons to clarify leadership and management expectations.

Additional reasons for clarifying leadership and management expectations include:

- Leadership and management should constitute a large portion of the work performed by leader/managers.
- Clarifying leadership and management expectations allows for unity of direction.

- Having a set of leadership and management expectations to work toward allows you as the leader to provide timely, relevant, and effective performance coaching.

- Having shared leadership and management expectations helps stem the natural tendency for most people to want to perform technical work over leadership and management. This is referred to as The Principle of Technical Priority.

The reasons for this technical preference include:

- The technical work is typically more tangible and provides more immediate and specific results feedback.

- Technical work is often more urgent, especially when compared to leadership.

- There is a fear of becoming technically obsolete unless one keeps their technical knowledge and skills up to date and honed.

- The leader/managers are unsure about just how to go about the work of leading and managing. There exists a lack of clarity, confidence, and competence. This is especially true for new leader/managers who are brand new in their leadership roles.

So, what is the antidote to counteract the effects of The Principle of Technical Priority?

The antidote is that: *Leaders need to make leader/managers lead and manage.*

They do so by:

- Clarifying, as discussed above, leadership and management expectations.

- Providing timely, relevant, and quality training and performance coaching.
- Making performance matter.

This is not the time nor place to go into depth on clarifying leadership and management results for specific positions. Our attention here is just to include Leadership and Management as part of Your Leadership Playing Field to list current responsibilities for this exercise.

However, if you are interested in how to go about crafting a position plan to define the reason a position or family of positions exists; that is, the role and set of results a position, and those reporting to it, if any, is organized to achieve, check out the *Clarity* building block section of my book *Building Commitment: Unleashing the Human Potential at Work*.[3] The other building blocks for building a culture of commitment are *Selection; Performance Coaching;* and *Growing Teams.*

Now that we have discussed these important clarifications and distinctions relative to accountability and responsibility, and leadership and management, we can move on to having you work on the exercise to help you identify potential opportunities to use more of your strengths or to use them to a greater degree in your current position.

PART I Scope Out Your Leadership Playing Field

What to Do

1. List your Key Result Areas. Your key areas of accountability and responsibility. Use the examples above as a guide. Use just a word or two for each KRA. Include Leadership and Management as a KRA.

2. Identify your responsibilities in each of the KRAs. That is, the work you should be personally performing in each of your KRAs.

PART II Mine Your Leadership Playing Field to Identify Possible Ways to Capitalize on Your Strengths

Review your list of current responsibilities and identify potential opportunities where you can use more of your strengths, or use them to a greater degree.

"What can I start doing . . . or do more of?"

PART III Plot Appropriate Implementation Strategies

1. Identify specific strategies for capitalizing on the opportunities you have identified.

2. Determine a logical sequence for capitalizing on your opportunities.

Freeing Up More Discretionary Time

In going through the exercise above perhaps you found some ways to capitalize on your strengths in your current leadership role. But I guess that, being a leader, your plate is already pretty full making it difficult to add any additional work, even if it is about capitalizing on your strengths. So, it is timely to look at possible ways to free up more discretionary time to allow you to implement your ideas by capitalizing on your strengths.

But even if you do not need to make some room to capitalize on your strengths, it makes good sense as a leader to always be on the alert to free up some more discretionary time to allow you to engage in greater value-added leadership work to achieve your organization's desired results.

Some Possible Strategies to Consider

For the work you are currently performing:

- **Discontinue**

    Is there any work or activities you are currently engaged in that really do not need to be done? Perhaps at one time, they were value-adding, but that is no longer the case.

- **Re-engineer the Work**

    Can the work or activity be streamlined? Is there a more efficient way to go about things?

- **Delegation Possibilities**

    - Are there any *ongoing* segments of work or activities that could be delegated?

    - Are there any routine or non-routine *time-limited* projects, activities, or duties that come your way that could be delegated?

    - Is there any work that you are holding on to just to keep your technical knowledge or skills honed? Or does that just make you feel good? Recall the Principle of Technical Priority discussed above.

In making any delegation, be it ongoing or time-limited work, or what you might consider to be routine or non-routine work, you need to assure that whomever you delegate the work to has the requisite *maturity level* to successfully perform the work. The maturity level is the responsibility or task-relevant competence and motivation to perform. If there is a knowledge of skill deficiency you need to provide timely and relevant training and performance coaching to upgrade the person's maturity level to satisfactorily perform the work.

The Art of Delegation

Delegating is a critical skill in performing your role as a leader/manager.

> **Delegation:** To entrust responsibility and authority to others and create accountability for results.

Delegating involves passing on to others either ongoing or time-limited responsibilities that you have performed or would normally perform.

Delegation is not:

- Passing the buck.
- Giving up your overall accountability.
- Refusing to decide by assigning it to another.
- Shirking personal responsibility.

For delegation to be truly effective, it needs to be looked at as an *investment*. An investment in that the delegation makes sense, and the person to whom you are making the delegation to has the maturity level, again the requisite competence and motivation, to succeed. And if they do not, you are going to see to it that they do.

When making the delegation, there are two components to consider: *intent* and *execution*.

Below is a comprehensive list of things to consider in making a delegation. The degree to which you discuss the items on this list will of course vary given the delegation's importance, complexity, uniqueness, and urgency; and, the responsibility or task-relevant maturity level of the person to whom the work or assignment is being delegated.

INTENT

The Situation (The Context)

- What is going on?

- Why this delegation?
- Why you?
- Why now?
- What are the "givens"?
  - Scope and boundaries.
  - Commitments and limitations.
    For example, resources and time.
- Who are the key stakeholders and players?

The "Whats"

- What is the objective?
- What are the desired outcomes? How do we know success when we see it?
- What is the timing?
- What are the concerns? What do we need to keep an eye on?

EXECUTION

The "Hows"

The work plan:

- Program
  - Steps
  - Responsibilities
- Schedule
- Resource Allocation
  - People-days
  - Financial
  - Space and Equipment
  - Information needed

The amount of discretion afforded to the person being delegated the work or assignment should depend on the responsibility or task-relevant maturity level of the person. Another important variable is the degree to which you need or want to stay involved. For example, even though the person you are making the delegation to has a high maturity level, you may want to stay involved because of the importance of the work being delegated, or the degree of knowledge and expertise you can bring to bear.

Regardless, a good practice is that after assuring the "Whats" are understood, make a deliberate decision as to how much discretion to allow for the person to formulate and execute the "Hows." Treat this point in the delegation as a dotted line, not a solid line.

Authority Level

The chart below provides a comprehensive list of authority levels for you to consider when delegating.

Figure 2.6 Levels of Authority When Delegating

Level of Authority	*Description*
Investigate	Look into the situation. Gather the data and report back to me. I'll decide what to do.
Recommend	Look into the situation and give me your thoughts on what to do. I will then decide what to do.
Decide and Get Approval	Examine the issue and decide what you are going to do, but do not act until you check with me first and get my approval.
Act and Inform	Decide what you think needs to be done; do it; and let me know how it turned out.
Act	Take action. No further contact with me is necessary.

Assistance Needed

- Is any special training or help needed?
- Are any advance communications with others needed regarding the delegation?
  - Who needs to know?
  - What do we need to tell them?
  - How are we going to tell them?

Working Together

- How are we going to work together regarding this delegation?
- What is the frequency and kind of interaction needed?

Managing Your Weaknesses

Earlier when working on *Discovering Your Strengths* we discussed the importance of identifying your weaknesses as well as strengths. That is, things you are not particularly good at or enthusiastic about.

Perhaps you can appropriately reduce your need to perform such work by applying the implementation strategies discussed earlier to free up more discretionary time. But most likely, there will continue to be responsibilities that you need to keep performing or should be performing, that you consider yourself to be weak at. Consequently, you will need to continue to perform these responsibilities the best you can, and not to avoid them or do less than you should.

If you need to increase your competencies regarding these responsibilities, you need to take reasonably prudent action to do so. Such improvement strategies as being mentored or coached; arranging for appropriate training; or, receiving ongoing support from others.

Committing to effectively manage your weaknesses may not result in converting them to strengths for you. But you will be more effective and efficient as a leader, and feel better about constructively addressing such deficiencies.

II

BEING A *SKILLFUL* SELF-AWARE LEADER

Now that we have worked through the *Self-Aware* portion of the title of the book, it is time to turn our attention to sharpening three critical interpersonal competencies to help you be a *Skillful* Self-Aware Leader.

These chapters aim to sharpen your skills in the perception, communication, and behavioral areas.

Chapter Three, *The Communication Process: Understanding the Basics*, provides a solid foundation for what is to follow.

The intent of Chapter Four, *Sharpening Your Perception: The Map Is Not the Territory*, is to help you increase your competence in accurately assessing just what is going on as you encounter important situations in everyday life.

Chapter Five, *The Structure of Magic: Skillfully Communicating about Differences*, helps you use effective listening and speaking communication patterns to seek to understand and be understood when encountering divergent points of view.

Chapter Six, *Using Natural and Adaptive Behaviors*, focuses on the importance to self-regulate and use both natural and adapted behaviors to pace with the situations, environments, and relationships you encounter.

3

THE COMMUNICATION PROCESS: UNDERSTANDING THE BASICS

The purpose of communication is to achieve shared understanding.

Talking is not communicating, and hearing is not listening.

While on the surface the communication process would seem to be rather straightforward. But a lot going on, as illustrated in Figure 3.1.

Figure 3.1: The Communication Process

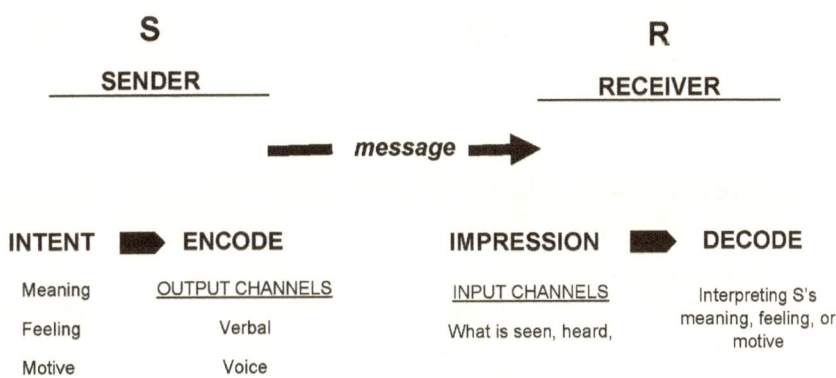

Let us briefly discuss the primary components of the communication process.

35

Intent

This is what you want to communicate. Your meaning, feeling, or motive, or all three.

Encode

You encode your messages by using the output channels, the three Vs—verbal, voice, and visual. They can each be described as follows:

- Verbal: The words. The content of the message.
- Voice: The tone, tempo, and inflections.
- Visual: Body language, expressions, gestures.

The voice and visual are commonly referred to as the nonverbals.

Impression

You initially receive messages via your input channels. What you see, hear, or feel. The impression is a fundamental activity between your nerve endings and what is going on. But even at this basic level differences arise. And you will perceive things differently from one instance to the next.

Decode

You decode the message by moving from what the sender says or does to your interpretation or translation of what the sender says or does. In simple conversation, they may be one and the same. But when the two are not in sync, it is important for you or the sender that you understand; you may need to enter into a conversation to gain clarity. And the work you may need to do to clear things up becomes a little, or a lot, more difficult when there are apparent or real differences between you and who you are attempting to communicate with.

With a basic knowledge of the communication process in tow, let us now discuss some important points for you to be aware of as a sender and receiver.

You as Sender

- It is important to *tailor your message* to your target audience, be it an individual or group. The more you know your audience the more you can communicate in a way that aligns with their interest, knowledge, and feelings regarding the subject of your communication.

- You need to *pace with your audience* by speeding up or slowing down the speed of your delivery. You want to continually do so by being observant of your receiver and his degree of attention. If he is with you, get on with it. But if he does not appear to be with you, you may need to slow down, test for interest or understanding by asking questions, or just listen and refrain from talking, or change the subject.

Relating to pacing, it is not only interesting but important to realize that there are significant *physiological differences* between the sender's ability to speak the words and the receiver's physical ability to hear the words. In general, the receiver can hear four times faster than the speaker. With his rudimentary voice box, to get the words out, in general, the speaker can go at a rate of 100–150 words per minute; whereas the receiver can hear at a rate of 450–600 words per minute.

An important caveat here. When talking, if you require your receiver to cycle back into her memory bank to call up something that relates to what you are communicating, be aware that this 4:1 ratio can quickly change. Suddenly you may leap ahead of your receiver. So be cognizant of your message and what you are requiring the receiver to do. And again, always be observant of your receiver to ascertain whether rather or not she is pacing with you.

- To your receiver, your *nonverbal communications (voice and visuals) are a powerful* component of your message. This is especially true when you are worked up about your message. So be aware of your nonverbals and amplify or diminish them to align with the message you want to deliver. If you want to emphasize your message in general or a particular aspect, perhaps raise your voice, or get more animated. By contrast, tone things down or become more still if called for. Your basic nature of course will have a lot to do with your tendency to amplify or diminish your messages.

As powerful as the nonverbals may be to the interpretation of a message, over the years there has been misinformation floating around the academic environment and beyond about greatly overstating the potency of the voice and visual output channels to the receiver. The claim has been that the meaning of the message is 7 percent verbal, 38 percent vocal, and 55 percent visual, meaning that 97 percent of the meaning of the message is nonverbal. This "7-55-38 formula" as it became to be known stemmed from research done in the 1960s by Albert Mehrabian and colleagues at the University of California at Los Angeles. This formula has since been debunked. The research had limitations and the research team has stated that their research was misunderstood. But the formula did get legs and you need to be aware of it just in case you have heard of it or come across it.[1]

Most of the messages we send or receive are straightforward and reliant mainly on the words spoken and received. The formula however does gain credence when we amp up the emotions on the part of either the sender or the receiver in a communications effort.

- It is important to *use the appropriate communication medium* when communicating your message. Think about the relationship between the output channels and the communication mediums you most commonly use as illustrated below:

Figure 3.2: Communication Mediums and Output Channels

Communication medium	Output channels involved
letter, fax, email, social media	Verbal
telephone, voicemail	Verbal + Voice
face-to-face, video conferencing, social media with video included	Verbal + Voice + Visual

The takeaway here is to use the appropriate communications medium that best fits your message, your audience, and the time required by the various mediums to formulate and deliver your message.

In so doing, you want to weigh the content of your message, your level of rapport with your audience, and the audience's knowledge of your subject. The more complex your subject, the more you want to use a communication medium that involves more than just the verbal. And the greater the rapport you have with your audience and their knowledge of your subject, the less you must worry about the communication medium used.

This all seems so basic. And it is. But you know of people and cases where the communication mediums are over or underused, or used inappropriately. For example, overusing email, including using it to transmit information that should be done in person.

And of course, there are instances when you will want to use a combination of mediums. For example, summarizing the results of a face-to-face meeting with some appropriate documentation.

- In *communicating important messages*:

    - *Embellish the content* of your message by *using appropriate examples* to clarify key points.

    - *Display appropriate emotion* to add your feelings to your meaning by making use of a) your voice output channel through varying the tone of your voice, the speed of delivery, and pausing; and, b) your visual output channel through using gestures and perhaps moving around.

    - In addition to using examples, *use symbolic language*[2] such as metaphors and stories to clarify key points.

- Most people have a preference in how they use the three senses of seeing, hearing, and feeling to take in (receive) and transmit (send) information. We all use all three senses, but most people have a preference. To some people, this preference is quite pronounced. The other two senses, smelling and tasting, do not play much of a role in communications unless those senses are called for to assess a task at hand, such as tasting a food item. Bandler and Grinder called this preference for favoring one of the three senses the *representational system*. They referred to the three senses as *visual* (seeing), *auditory* (hearing), and *kinesthetic* (feeling).[3] A person with kinesthetic preferences values experiencing things.

With people you interact with frequently, you should be able to pick out these preferences if indeed they do exist. Tune into the kinds of words people use consistently.

For example:

- *"I see your point."*
  "But that is only my view."
  (Visual)

- *"Sounds good to me."*
  "At least that's what I hear."
  (Auditory)

- *"I think I have a good feel for what you are trying to say."*
  "My experience has always been that . . . "
  (Kinesthetic)

In serious conversation, the value of knowing one's preferred representational system allows you to align with your receiver's preferred system when speaking to enhance rapport and gain clarity.

When addressing a group in making important announcements or in training experiences you want to attempt to incorporate all three representational systems into your communications. You can do so by perhaps reinforcing the words with handouts, using visual aids, and involving your audience by having them do something.

- In like manner, most people have preferred natural thinking and behavioral preferences or styles. Most times, because they are a natural part of a person, such preferences occur at a subconscious level.

  Even though you may not be familiar with the two individual assessment instruments briefly described below, they help you understand the nature of these natural preferences.

The *Myers-Briggs Type Indicator* focuses on character and temperament.[4]

Its structure consists of four pairs of preferences:

Extraversion vs. Introversion

Intuition vs. Sensation (the facts)

Thinking vs. Feeling

Judging (closure) vs. Perceiving (open options)

The *DISC* assessment focuses on behavioral style. Its four styles are:

Behavioral Style		Description/Preferences
D	Dominance	Driver; results; assertive; action; bottom line; control; independence; decisive.
I	Influencing	Relationships; people; persuasive; seeks approval; dislikes structure.
S	Steadiness	Progress; collaboration; stability; teamwork; harmony; staying the course.
C	Conscientiousness	Security; stability; proven; thorough; facts; assurance; patient; standards.

Although I am not promoting these two popular assessments, they are good at what they deliver for the general population.[1] There are other types of assessments, for example, leadership, organizational, sales, and learning assessments, that are designed for specific audiences or purposes.

Although such frameworks can be very useful, they are not essential for you to better understand the thinking and behavioral preferences of people you interact with frequently. Just pay attention.

The value once again of identifying such preferences is that in important conversations you can gain greater rapport and be more effective, no matter what your natural thinking and behavioral preferences are, *by aligning with the thinking and behavioral preferences* of whomever you are interacting with. Think of yourself as a rubber band stretching out to meet the person you are interacting with.

Stereotype Mode

Based on his research, Glen Strasburg, Professor-Emeritus at the University of California, Los Angeles and California State University, East Bay posited that most people use definite verbal, voice, or visual patterns to signal when they have had enough of the conversation and want to bale. What happens, he describes, is that the crispness of one's perception diminishes as one experiences accumulative units of stress or boredom. That makes sense. But what is interesting is that rather than slowly continuing a downward trajectory, the bottom suddenly falls out. And the person so indicates by exhibiting what is for them a stereotype mode by using a personal pattern of verbal, voice, and visual signals.

---

[1] If you are interested in learning more about either of these two assessments discussed above refer to the Endnotes at the back of the book for Chapter Three, footnote 4.

Figure 3.3: Stereotype Mode

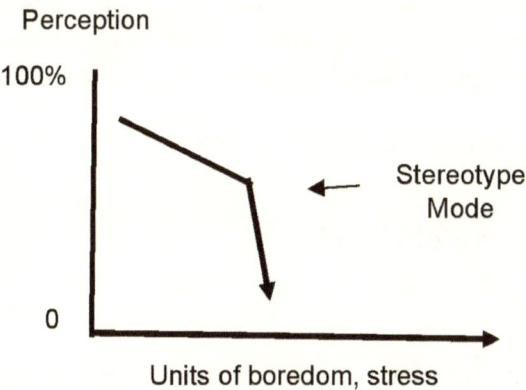

For most people, if indeed they have a stereotype mode, they are unaware of it. When I first became aware of this phenomenon, I asked my staff for some feedback. It was an office setting. They said that I displayed such a mode when I had enough. And what I did is turn to my right and fiddle with papers on my desk.

So what value was such feedback to me? It was very valuable. Because when I felt myself slipping into my stereotype mode, I could course correct and get re-engaged. That, of course, is assuming I wanted to. And if I did not want to get re-engaged, the better alternative was to express that I had enough.

Do you know your stereotype mode? If not, are you interested in discovering it?

If so, work with an adult friend or friends. Adult friends are better sources of feedback than family members. Family members will most likely be hesitant to provide you with honest feedback because they are too close to you and fearful of harming the relationship. Explain the stereotype mode to an adult friend and ask for their feedback. Then thank them.

You as Receiver

There is a lot to say about you as a receiver, but that is saved for Chapter 4 which focuses on perception, and Chapter 5 which focuses on effective communication patterns in communicating about differences.

But this is a good time to talk about levels of listening.

Figure 3.4: Levels of Listening

1 Ignore

- Non-listening; tune out, consciously or unconsciously.
- The message: *"I don't care"* or *"You're not important."*

2 Passive Listening

- Very common.
- To many listening means "be there and be quiet."
- Often frustrating because of the lack of feedback.

3 Selective Listening

- Listen to what we want to listen to.
- When one determines to be interested, one may function at Level 4 (Attentive Listening) or Level 5 (Active Listening). When one determines not to be interested, one may function at Level 2 (Passive Listening) or Level 1 (Non-Listening).
- The problem at this level is that as listeners we are inconsistent and judgmental.

4 Attentive Listening

Tuned in, interested, and participating. But the focus is only on the content or facts of the message and not the emotion. At this level can tell you what you said, but not necessarily what you meant.

5 Active Listening

Listen in a manner that shows care and respect. Seek to understand the total message, that is, meaning, feeling, and motive, by participating and demonstrating understanding.

Active listening is thoroughly covered in Chapter 5. This is the type of listening you want to do when the speaker really wants you to understand, you really want to understand, or you both want to assure shared understanding occurs.

As effective and essential as it is in attempting to achieve understanding, you will not want to be an active listener continuously. What? For one thing, you will be a big bore and people will avoid you. For another, active listening is hard work and can be exhausting. You need to concentrate and track with the speaker, demonstrate that you are seeking to understand, and check out your understanding through inquiry, paraphrasing, and speculating about the speaker's real meaning, feeling, and motive. That is a lot. So, you need to pick your spots. The topic and the needs of the sender and yourself will determine when that is. And with good active listening skills, it will become easier and certainly be worth it.

Communication Barriers

Exercise 3.1:   Identifying Communication Barriers

Purpose

Heighten your awareness of all the things that get in the way of achieving understanding in the communication process. And with a greater awareness be able to minimize your creation of such obstacles.

What to Do

1. Take a few moments, and on a sheet of paper jot down verbal, vocal, and visual behaviors that can get in the way of communications between a sender and receiver.

2. Compare your list with the list in Appendix A: Perception and Communications: Answers and Comments.

There are no right or wrong answers. Nor is the intent to have either of the two lists exhaustive. The intent is to raise your awareness a bit so you will be better prepared to avoid creating such barriers and to self-correct when you catch yourself engaging in such behaviors.

Where We Are

In this chapter, we looked at the communication process and all that is going on between a sender and receiver. With all that is going on, it makes one marvel at just how well we communicate most times without a lot of effort. But issues arise when the heat is turned up and differences arise. The balance of this section is intended to help you communicate effectively in such instances.

In the next chapter, Chapter 4, *Perception: The Map Is Not the Territory,* we explore perception as you most likely have never experienced before. The goal is to sharpen your perceptive skills to assess "what is going on"? especially when it comes to having differences.

Then in Chapter 5, *The Structure of Magic: Skillfully Communicating about* Differences, using your perceptive skills, we look at using effective listening and speaking communication patterns to help you: a) seek to understand and be understood; and, as called for b) decide on "what's possible?"; and c) determine the next steps to move things to a new and better place.

4

SHARPENING YOUR PERCEPTIVE SKILLS: THE MAP IS NOT THE TERRITORY

"The map is not the territory."

—Alfred Korzybski

"Everyone is 'right' by his or her definition."

—Alfred Korzybski

The work of Alfred Korzybski,[1] Sam Bois,[2] S.I. Hayakawa,[3] and William H. Pemberton[4] drives a lot of what we discuss in this and the following chapter. They are pioneers in the field of general semantics. General semantics (or semantics) is the theory and study of the human evaluative process.

The late William H. Pemberton was a dear friend and mentor. Bill, in addition to being a general semanticist, was a psychologist. He provided so much wisdom to impart regarding the human evaluative process and communicating about differences.

You have a unique window of the world. Everyone does. It is through this window that you see and process what is going on (WIGO). It determines how the world shows up for you.

Your view of the world is just that—your view of the world. Reality is out there. Reality is WIGO. And you are an interpreter of WIGO. You make your own unique translation of WIGO. Alfred Korzybski captured this critical perception so well with his phrase *"The map is not the territory."* The territory is out there in the real world. That is, "what he said"; "what they did"; "who she is"; and so forth. As you experience WIGO you become a mapmaker. The accuracy of your mapmaking will stray from reality a little bit, or quite a lot, depending on a variety of factors. Such factors as your interest and knowledge relative to WIGO; the complexity of WIGO; and, your personal makeup and experiences. Your core and your mental models.

Having established the importance of this perception principle of "the map is not the territory," let us move on and get you involved. Exercise 4.1 below is the first exercise on a journey through this chapter on perception.

LEADERSHIP BEGINS WITH YOU

Exercise 4.1: What Do You See?

What to Do

1. Look at the three images below[5] and note what you see.
2. Turn to Appendix A: "Perception and Communication: Answers and Comments." to compare notes.

Exercise 4.1 involves an activity between your visual nerve endings and each of the three sketches. It is an example of the basic level of perception which involves observing WIGO by using one of several of your senses: seeing, hearing, feeling tasting, or smelling. In this instance, seeing.

Working with Bill Pemberton in providing training sessions on communicating about differences, he would often get the attendees involved using their tasting sense.

He would use small strips of paper that had been dipped ahead of time in a solution of phenyl-thio-carbamide. Each person was asked to wad their small strip of paper up and swish it around in their mouth. People were then asked to talk about their experiences. Some people tasted the paper as bitter, and some tasted nothing. Turns out that whether they are a taster or not comes with the gene. We will discuss the participants' various responses to their experiences a bit later in conjunction with a valuable model that lays out the stages of personal mental development in the human evaluative process.

Let's look at another example below.[6] This time involving the sense of feeling.

These experiments in perception involve only making maps of the territory using one of your senses. I can attest that people can and often do get gotten quite worked up at this fundamental level, arguing about who had the right map.

When we move beyond the sensory or observation level and people begin to make broader maps using their unique makeups and beliefs, you can appreciate that the differences in interpretations become much more diverse. And when there is some ownership or emotion involved regarding the accuracy of mapmaking going on, you can further appreciate how the task of communicating about differences becomes a lot more difficult. That is why we are here.

Now let us go to the next exercise and ratchet things up a notch.

Exercise 4.2: Who Done It?[7]

What to Do

1. Read the brief story below. Assume that all the information in the story is accurate and true. You may refer back to the story if you wish.
2. Read each statement about the story. Determine whether each statement is:

    "T" – True
    "F" – False
    "?" – Not sure

    Circle your choice.

3. Turn to Appendix A: Perception and Communication: "Answers and Comments" to check your answers.

STORY

Babe Smith has been killed. Police have rounded up six suspects, all of whom are known gangsters. All of them are known to have been near the scene of the killing at the approximate time that it occurred. All had substantial motives for wanting Smith killed. However, one of these suspected gangsters, Slinky Sam, has positively been cleared of guilt.

STATEMENTS ABOUT STORY

1. Slinky Sam is known to have been near the scene of the killing of Babe Smith.   T   F   ?
2. All six of the rounded-up gangsters were known to have been near the scene of the crime.   T   F   ?
3. Only Slinky Sam has been cleared of guilt.   T   F   ?
4. All six of the rounded-up suspects were near the scene of Smith's killing at the approximate time it took place.   T   F   ?
5. The police do not know who killed Smith.   T   F   ?
6. All six suspects are known to have been near the scene of the foul deed.   T   F   ?
7. Smith's murderer did not confess of his own free will.   T   F   ?
8. Slinky Sam was not cleared of guilt.   T   F   ?
9. It is known that the six suspects were in the vicinity of the cold-blooded assassination.   T   F   ?

How did you do? Review your answers by turning to Appendix A. But do not fret over it. This exercise is designed to have you distinguish between fact and inference.

THE LADDER OF INFERENCE

The exercise above provides a perfect transition for introducing an extremely valuable structure—The Ladder of Inference. The Ladder of Inference helps you develop an awareness of the various levels of inference or mapmaking you might engage in as you perceive what is going on.

Figure 4.1: The Ladder of Inference

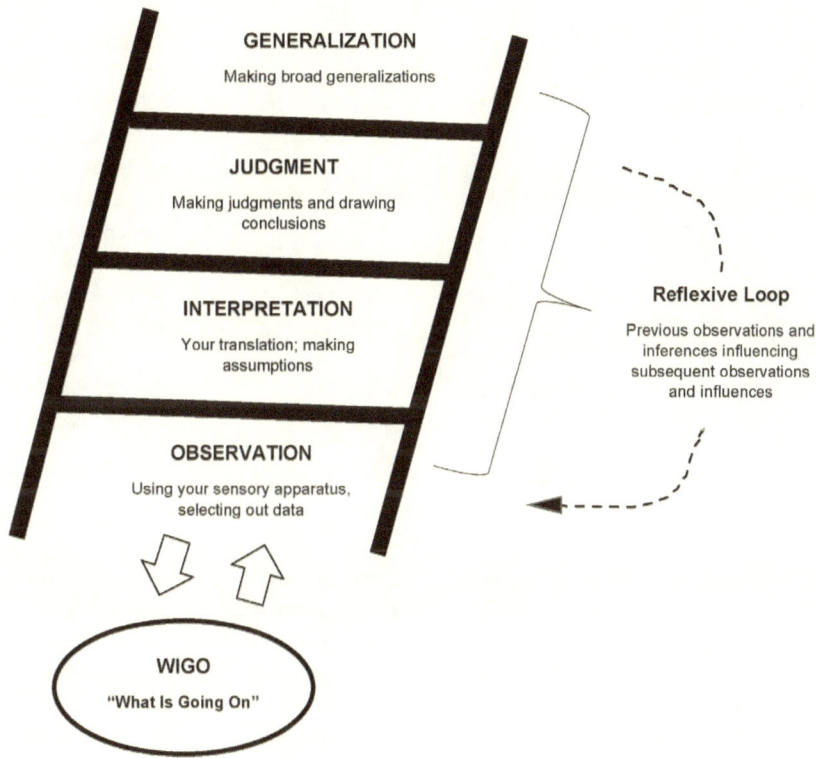

The Ladder of Inference demonstrates that as you ascend the various rungs of the ladder you make broader and broader maps of the territory, that is, WIGO. You go from sensing to postulating; from facts to assumptions. At the observation level, your map may be very detailed. As you move beyond your sensory apparatus and factor more and more of you as a person into the evaluative process your map becomes sketchier. There is nothing wrong with this. It is natural. Even though your higher-level maps of inference will be increasingly more general, you still could be spot on with reality. Or, you may increasingly miss the mark as you ascend the rungs. But that is the beauty of this construct. It helps you be aware of your level of inferences. And, validate your assumptions.

Figure 4.2: Examples: The Ladder of Inference

	Example 1	Example 2	Example 3
Generalization	John is unreliable.	No wonder the rates are so high.	Mary can't keep up the pace, and so she's willing to have us lose our competitive edge.
Judgment	John always comes in late.	That is so nonproductive.	She can't compete very well.
Interpretation	John knew exactly when the meeting was to start. He deliberately came in late.	Must be a poor job of planning.	Mary doesn't like competition.
Observation	The meeting was called for 9 a.m. and John came at 9:30. He didn't say why he was late.	Look, there is a utility construction crew. One guy is working and the other three are standing around.	Mary says: "We need to find a way to reward people for the contribution they make to the whole."

WIGO

In addition to serving as a useful construct to increase your understanding of the various levels of inference, The Ladder of Inference can be valuable to you in communicating key thoughts. Toward this end, the ladder can be thought of as representing various levels of abstraction from specific to general. It is important to *vary the level of abstraction* in your communications when you are trying to make a point. That is, to go from the specific, such as data and facts, to the general, such as conclusions and generalizations, and vice versa. To go from discussing DNP (Domestic National Product) to talking about meat and potatoes (marketplace elements that go into make up the DNP).

Figure 4.3: Varying Your Level of Abstraction

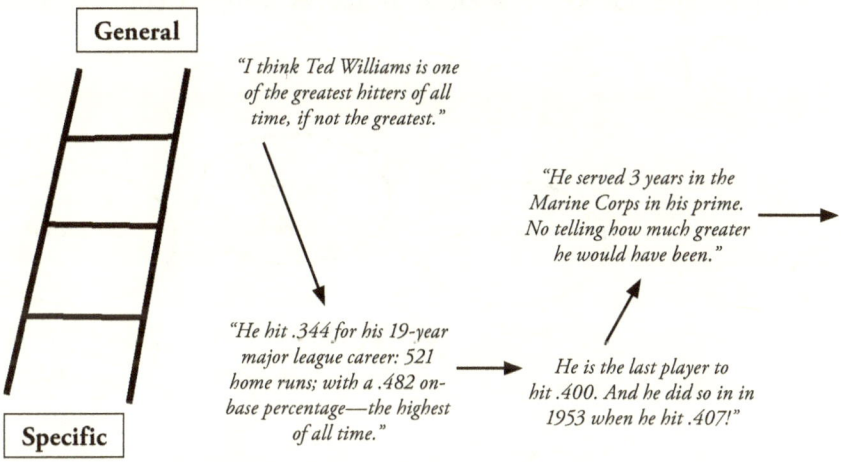

When you receive feedback like, "What's your point?" you are being asked to be more general, to summarize. When you hear "Give me an example," you are being asked to be more specific. In such instances, people are asking you to vary your level of abstraction to help them understand what you are trying to communicate. That is useful feedback.

Let us now turn our attention to further your understanding as to why you and everyone else have unique windows of the world and consequently make different maps of the same territory.

CARL WELTE

THE STRUCTURE OF INTERPRETATION

Figure 4.4: Structure of Interpretation

The Structure of Interpretation helps you understand and appreciate how the world shows up for you, and others.

The general semanticists referenced earlier, Korzybski, Bois, Hayakawa, and Pemberton, used the term Structural Differential to refer to this human evaluative model. I prefer the term Structure of Interpretation. I believe it to be a more descriptive label. I have also redesigned the model and added a few embellishments, which I consider to be enhancements.

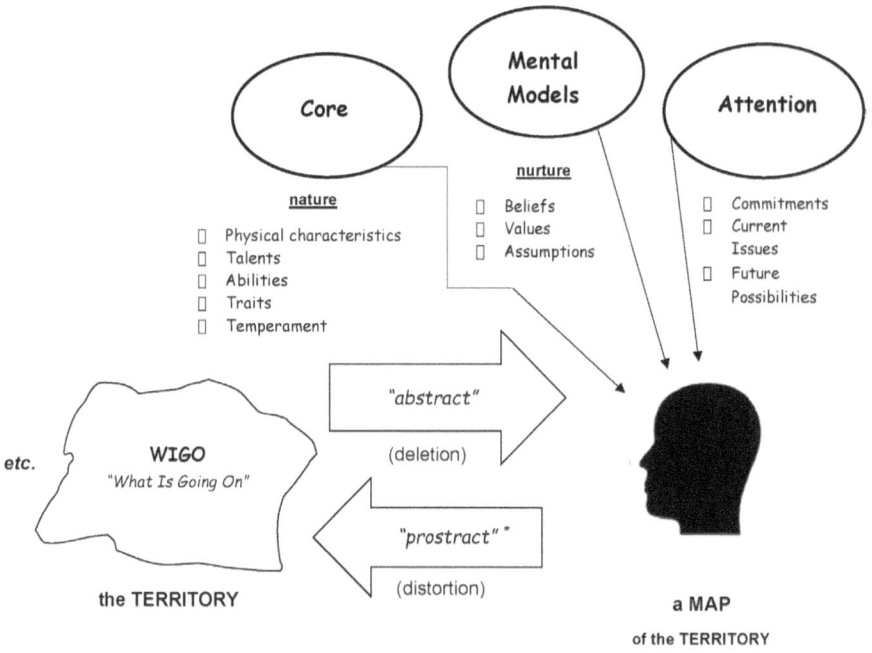

---

* Pemberton coined the word *prostract* to represent the fact that we project ourselves into our viewing of what is going on.

Understanding the Structure of Interpretation

The fact that reality and your perception of reality are two different things has been stressed, and will continue to be. This perception principle is emphasized so heavily because it is so pivotal for you to be able to engage in genuine and effective dialogue regarding differences you encounter. Again, the "map is not the territory" metaphor is used to summarize this critical perception principle.

The Structure of Interpretation model allows us to dive into some detail to better understand this principle. That is, how we view and process WIGO.

Let us now review the components of the model.

Abstracting and Prostracting

The Ladder of Inference demonstrates how you can have varying levels of inference as you take in WIGO. These inferences start at the observation level and can progress to broader levels of assumptions and judgments as you ascend The Ladder of Inference.

The phenomenon of abstracting and prostracting adds to your understanding of what happens when you take in information in your mapmaking process.

When you *abstract* from the territory you form your personal map of WIGO. In the process of making your map, you *delete* some, or a lot, of what is really going on. The amount of deletion depends on such factors as the complexity of the territory, your relevant knowledge, your interest, and your core and mental models.

You also *prostract* or push yourself into WIGO in making your map. That is, project your core and mental models into the territory. In the process of doing so, you *distort* a little or a lot of what is actually going on.

Do not worry, there is nothing wrong about you deleting or distorting. It just happens and is natural. Of course, with people who grossly delete or distort society needs to step in and attend to them.

Exercise 4.3: Deletion

What to Do

1. Count the number of Fs in the statement below.
2. Turn to Appendix A: Perception and Communication: "Answers and Comments" to check your response.

> FINISHED FILES ARE THE RESULT OF
> YEARS OF SCIENTIFIC STUDY COMBINED
> WITH THE EXPERIENCE OF YEARS.

Exercise 4.4: Distortion

What to Do

1. Describe what you see in the picture below.
2. Turn to Appendix A: Perception and Communication: "Answers and Comments" to check your response.

etc. is shown in the model to signify that there is always something more to be seen, heard, known, or said about anything.

Core and Mental Models

We covered Core and Mental Models in detail in Chapter One when we looked at the Dimensions of the Inner You. So, we will not say any more here.

Attention

What is on your mind, be it "in the moment" or long-term issues, concerns, hopes, ambitions, or commitments also affect your perception of WIGO. And it cuts both ways.

If you are currently keenly interested in something and that subject is being discussed you perk up and tune in. Conversely, your preoccupation with something that is on your mind can substantially interfere with your understanding of WIGO as you tune out, temporarily or completely.

Level of Consciousness

An understanding and use of the Structure of Interpretation can greatly increase your Level of Consciousness.

I defined this important concept at the beginning of this chapter. I will do so again here.

> **Level of Consciousness:** The degree to which one is aware of self and others, and uses such awareness to enhance communications and relationships.

Daniel Goleman uses the term emotional intelligence in his pioneering and valuable work to refer to this important concept I call the level of consciousness.[8] Goleman argues that emotional intelligence can matter more than raw intelligence in determining one's human effectiveness. In other words, EQ (Emotional Quotient) can be more important than IQ (Intelligence Quotient).

As expressed earlier, I prefer the term level of consciousness in understanding and explaining this important concept. I do not mean to be picky, but the word "emotional" is a little bit narrow for me in relating to this concept. Also, the word "intelligence" can be confusing in that it relates to the brain. Whereas, "consciousness" relates to awareness and feelings.

Call the concept whatever you wish. The important thing is to understand and appreciate the concept.

STAGES OF AWARENESS

In interacting with the world, you run into a variety of folk with different levels of tolerance and viewpoints that differ from yours. On one end of the spectrum, you run into people who are locked into their maps. On the other end of the spectrum, some are tolerant and respectful of divergent points of view, in general, or relating to a specific topic. They are willing to revise their maps based on new realities, new learning, or reaching a higher level of consciousness. We are not talking about "wishy-washy" people here. Or what politicians call "flip-flopping" when they want to demean other politicians because they altered their views on an issue.

In Chapter One you were encouraged to adopt a *growth mindset* as contrasted with a *fixed mindset*. It is timely to bring this important point up again. Carol Dweck in her book *Mindset* uses the term *fixed mindset* to refer to those who are not open to divergent points of view and learning. She uses the term *growth mindset* to refer to those who are open to new and different inputs, divergent points of view, continuous learning, and perhaps changing their way of thinking based upon such inputs and experiences.[9]

Pemberton with a model he calls the Sanity Spectrum allows us to deepen our understanding regarding the various developmental stages that exist in the human evaluative process.[10] I use the label Stages of

Awareness in referring to this important human development model. It is shown in the chart below.

Figure 4.5: Level of Consciousness: Stages of Awareness

Stage	Personal Mental Development	Philosophical Viewpoint or Orientation	Personal Identification	Handling Conflict
I	Infant Sensing Dependence	There are no other viewpoints.	"me"	Withdraw
II	Child *"You're OK... I'm not OK"* Classifying Dependence	**ABSOLUTISTIC** Two-valued orientation: either/or; right/wrong; good/bad, etc. The quality is in the thing.	"like me"	"One way"
III	Youth/Parent *"I'm OK... you're not OK"* Relating Independence	**RELATIVISTIC** I determine what is real, best, right, good, etc. I determine the quality.	"like us"	"Many ways—but, one right way"
IV	Adult *"I'm OK... you're OK"* [11] Postulating Interdependence	**TRANSITORY** Multi-valued orientation. The map is not the territory. It is just a map.	"like anyone"	"Many ways—so let's compare notes and come up with the best way."

This is a powerful and robust model. It says a lot.

Let us enliven the model and deepen your understanding of it by using a real-life example.

We draw upon the example used earlier in this chapter. To review, Pemberton used chemically treated paper wads and had group participants chew on a wad and discuss their experiences. To some, the paper tasted bitter. To others it was tasteless. Whether a person was a taster or not came with the gene.

The exercise was used to emphasize the map is not the territory perception principle. We will now look at the typical sorts of responses the participants had to illustrate the differences between Stages II, III, and IV in the evaluative process as shown in the Stages of Awareness model.

Figure 4.6: "Bitter" or "Not Bitter"?: Stage of Awareness Responses

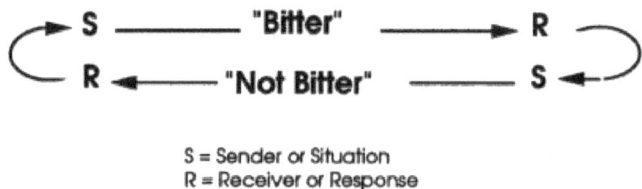

S = Sender or Situation
R = Receiver or Response

See the typical responses below based on the various Stages of Awareness.

Stage of Awareness Responses to the Experiment

Stage I   Not part of the exercise.

                           They would not be able to relate to WIGO.

Stage II   The quality is in the thing. Therefore, the taste is in
Absolutistic   the chemical.

                           Interpretation: The other person is lying; or has
                                             a different piece of paper; or has
                                             faulty taste buds.

                           Standard talk: "Go back and taste it again."

Stage III   The taste is determined by me.
Relativistic
                           Interpretation: We may be different.

                           Standard talk: "No big deal; I'm telling it the way
                                             it is."

Stage IV   There is an interesting transaction going on
Transitory   here between the chemical on the paper and the
                           participant's taste buds.

                           Interpretation: Curious if we are different, and if
                                             so, I wonder why.

                           Standard talk: "I did/did not taste it. How about
                                             you? What is going on?"

With your understanding of the Stages of Awareness model, you realize that the lower the development stage of the person you are interacting with, the tougher the communication challenge. A person with a fixed mindset, either in general or issue-specific, is not interested or capable of engaging in a genuine conversation on the subject. They typically go into flight or fight mode. And if they do enter a discussion, it usually will be in the form of a debate, not a conversation.

This is a good place to identify and define the different kinds of interactions that can occur.

Figure 4.7: Categories of Interaction

	Debate	**Discussion** or **Conversation**	**Dialogue**
Intent	To change another's views or assumptions. To win.	To come to some sort of closure, whether we agree or not. Or fully understand one another.	Seek to understand one another's meaning, feelings, or motive. Explain; discover; develop insight.
Meaning	"to beat down"	"to shake apart"	"to turn together"

Monologue: One-way communications. Duologue: Simultaneous monologues.

The ground rules for effective dialogue include:

- Treat each other as colleagues.
- People will not have remarks attributed to them outside our conversation unless we agree to it.
- Right and wrong are not a concern.
- Injection of new perspectives is encouraged.
- No sarcasm.
- Treat everyone with respect.

Korzybski maintained that we slip away from sanity to the degree we fail to make distinctions between different levels of abstracting as we make our maps. He laid this out on a hypothetical distribution as shown below with most people at Stages II and III.[12]

Figure 4.8: Korzybski's Sanity Model

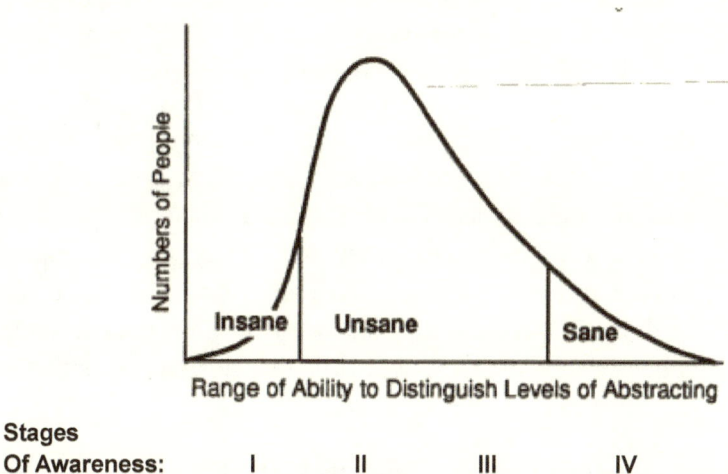

Using Korzybski's Sanity Model as a focus, let us explore some of the implications.

- A young child typically cannot interact beyond Stage I when differences occur. *"It's mine!" "No, it's mine!"*

- As the child ages, hopefully, she will grow mentally as well as physically. To go from Stage II to Stage III, and hopefully to Stage IV. This of course takes time. Moving beyond a fixed mindset toward a growth mindset involves getting to know oneself and developing the requisite level of consciousness, along with skillful communication.

- Some people may not have the ability to grow beyond Stage I or Stage II.

- Other people, for whatever reason, may opt to stay at Stage II, electing not to continuously learn and grow. Most times this occurs at a subconscious level.

They may feel comfortable in what they perceive to be a sheltered environment and not have their assumptions challenged or need to revise them in light of new and emerging realities. They will tend to surround themselves with people "like me" or "like us" and otherwise become withdrawn.

- As we live our lives, we all form allegiances with people and groups. Hopefully, these associations give us satisfaction and perhaps help us learn and grow. But for some people, these associations stifle who they are. They are not open and honest amid such affiliations. They are fearful that if they are authentic, open, and honest, they will suffer the consequences. They will be embarrassed, ridiculed, lose status, suffer career consequences, or be ostracized.

- And going a step, or several steps, further, some people become so consumed with individuals and groups that such affiliations become a large part of their identity. Anyone or anything that rubs up against such affiliations the wrong way is seen as the enemy. So sad.

So, what is to be done to help individuals engulfed in the last situation described? When who they are is largely defined by such unhealthy associations and they become blinded to any countervailing opinions. They shut down.

Most of these folks are otherwise intelligent and you would think they could see what they got themselves into. And the fact of the matter is that most of them do. Think about the people you see, hear, or read about in public view who you know are lying, and they do too. What will it take for them to get real?

For some of them, education and enlightenment may work. But for most, until the driving forces to change outweigh the restraining forces to hang on to such beliefs, regardless if they believe them or not, they will not change. They fear too much for their own hides rather than risk doing the right thing for the greater good.

So, what should your role be in trying to help these people see the light? Probably nothing. Unless you think that shedding a little enlightenment might be helpful. But do not overdo it. People do not want to be told how to think and what to do. If they do see themselves clearly and have the necessary fortitude and courage, they can move themselves forward. But, you can do good in your own sphere of influence and have a positive effect by modeling the way through you demonstrating your level of consciousness.

The same thing needs to be said about nudging the hypothetical distribution curve in the sanity model to the right. Few of us are going to be able to have a large impact overall. But locally there is hope. And as you model the way at the local level, that is your family, friends, and community, you may have an impact far greater than you think. But do not wait for people to come up and say "Thanks for helping me raise my level of consciousness." That is just not the way it works most times.

In the next chapter, we discuss and practice effective listening and speaking communication patterns to be used in communicating about differences. These communication patterns allow you to capably demonstrate a high level of consciousness in seeking to understand and be understood. Hopefully, these effective communication patterns will become more and more a part of you and help you grow into an even better you.

But the material covered in this chapter is critical if you are going to genuinely communicate about differences. A lack of authenticity is easily detected. And no matter how adept you are at communication, your talk is likely to be perceived as being mechanical and not caring. And that you are not really seeking to understand or to be understood.

5

THE STRUCTURE OF MAGIC: SKILLFULLY COMMUNICATING ABOUT DIFFERENCES

"There is not much you can't say if you say it right."

—Carl Welte

The Principle of Reciprocity (or Caring)*: "If you think I am trying to understand you, you just may be indebted to try and understand me."*

—William Pemberton

To effectively communicate about differences or any important communications, the lessons in this chapter regarding using skillful communication patterns need to be applied in conjunction with the lessons of the preceding chapter about skillfully assessing just what is going on. That is, you use a high level of consciousness to accurately assess just what is going on, but you also need to effectively use listening and speaking communication patterns to move things to new and better places.

Likewise, if you are knowledgeable regarding the mechanics of effective communication, but are not perceptive regarding what is going on, or do not care, your communication will be just that—mechanical. Your communication will be perceived as hackneyed and insincere. And you may come across as phony. Your communication seems to be coming right out of a book, and not the heart. *Both effective perception and communication skills are needed to seek to understand and be understood.*

Getting Grounded: Three Recommendations

A good place to start before exploring the skillful communication patterns that are critical to meaningful conversations is to provide three recommendations to help you get focused on any important conversations that come your way.

1. The 3Rs of Effective Communication

You need to be mindful of this first recommendation whenever you communicate about differences. The construct comes from Bill Pemberton.

Figure 5.1: The 3 Rs of Effective Communication

Role	• "What is my role in this situation?" • "Should I leave well enough alone; or, would directly addressing the issue be appropriate?" • "What are my authorities in this situation?" "Can I can make anything happen?" "Can I influence?" If I cannot influence, drop it. • "Speak up now or at some other opportune time?" • "Who are the key stakeholders?" • "What are the consequences of doing nothing?"
Risk	Good communication is risky. You never know what you are going to find or where things might go when you seek to understand and be understood and be authentic about yourself in doing so. To effectively deal with resistance and differences, you must be willing to take a risk and have the time and effort to actively listen and assertively communicate.
Responsibility	Being willing and able to clean up any messes you might create by reaching out to effectively address questions and issues and being authentic in doing so. You want to approach the interaction with a "win-win" or "both/and" versus a "win-lose" or zero-sum attitude. What you are trying to do is get the real issues out on the table and see what is possible. In doing so, you will use your communication skills to try and keep both you and the others you are interacting with whole.

2. Freeze Frame

The second recommendation is a technique to be used "in the moment." It is applied whenever you are about to engage in important communication. You take a quick time out and get yourself centered. You get yourself to neutral by closing your eyes, literally or figuratively, and taking a few deep breaths. You do this before such instances as making an important phone call or speaking up about your concerns at a meeting.

Once you begin to incorporate this practice into your normal routine you will be surprised how quickly you can get centered, including in the middle of a meeting. The term "freeze frame"[1] is a good descriptor of what you want to accomplish in calling your brief time out. Because what you are doing is stopping the action right on the set, sort of speak to, get collected.

3. Communication Plan

A third recommendation is, whenever you have time to prepare for a difficult conversation, outline your communication plan by thinking through the following:

- What is my objective?
- What is my strategy?
    - Basic approach.
    - Key messages.
    - When and where to have the communication.
    - Who should be present?
    - What is/are the natural behavioral styles of the person/people I will be meeting with? What is the best way to adapt to such styles?
- Communication patterns.
    - Think about what you want to say and how to say it.
    - Think about possible reactions and how to prepare for such reactions.

- Do not get too scripted, however. You do not want to come off as being canned. And, once you get started with the meeting it may go places you have not anticipated. You need to be flexible.

TALK CHAIN

The talk chain is a very valuable construct. It serves well in helping to introduce communication patterns. Communication patterns can either hinder or help effective communication.

Figure 5.2: Talk Chain

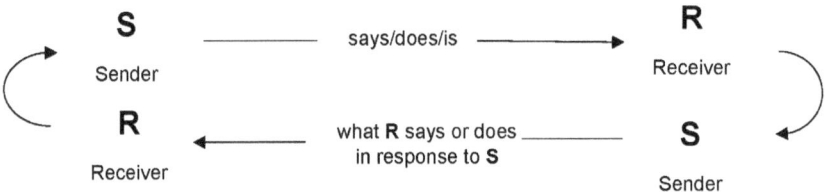

If R is okay with what or who S says, does, or is, or WIGO (What Is Going On), everything is okay. But if R is insulted or knocked off balance by what S says, does, or is, or WIGO, then how R responds is pivotal as to whether the talk chain stays open and whether any constructive communication can occur.

But before discussing ineffective and effective communication patterns in tough situations, let us take a quick, but very much related, detour.

Principles or laws from various people are scattered throughout this book. "The map is not the territory," the invaluable principle that anchored the last chapter, is an example. These sage sayings say a lot in a few words and serve to highlight and summarize the topic being discussed.

Below are some laws relating to our current focus.

Law of Insult: *I am a partial author of any insult I give or receive.*

—William H. Pemberton

(I do not know. Maybe my standards are too finicky. Or maybe it is the way I came across.)

Law of Choice: *It may be wrong for me to assume that a person could have behaved any differently in a given situation.*

—William H. Pemberton

(Who knows? If I was in his shoes, I may have done the same thing.)

Law of Assumed Benevolence: *It is probably safe to assume that most people do not want to intentionally insult or hurt me.*

—Dan Fischer

(They have enough problems of their own.)

Figure 5.3 lists natural responses and skilled responses in communicating about differences.

Figure 5.3: Natural and Skilled Responses

<u>Natural Responses Can Hinder</u>

Responses that tend to get in the way of constructively talking about differences

- <u>Sullen</u> silence
- Attack
- Deceiving

<u>Skilled Responses Can Help</u>

Responses that can facilitate meaningful conversation about differences

Active Listening

- Attending and Acknowledging
- Inquiry
- Paraphrasing/Speculating

Assertive Communication

- Describing
- Stating Thoughts
- Stating Feelings

Natural Responses

Pemberton identified the three typical natural responses shown in Figure 5.3 above of people in crisis and labeled these responses as the Sad Syndrome. "SAD" is formed by taking the first letter of each of the three typical responses. And if that is all a person can do in uncomfortable situations, that is, clam up, whack back, or make a joke, it is indeed sad.

Figure 5.4: Natural Responses in Crisis

Sullen silence	"anger-inners" "clamming up" "copping-out" pouting child passive-aggressive Contrasted with the silence of listening
Attack	"anger-outers" whacking back judgments; advice; blaming "YOU" messages
Deceiving	fraud; phony; making light incongruities between feeling and talk passive-aggressive

The big problem with these natural responses in crisis is that they tend to invalidate or cancel out the other person. And in so doing, such natural responses are likely to trigger natural responses on the part of the other person. The net effect is that the talk chain shuts down.

Principle of Imbalance (or Hyperexis):	*The very thing I do when insulted or knocked off balance emotionally or psychologically to get myself back in balance often makes things worse.*

—William H. Pemberton

Hyperexis is a Greek word meaning "fever." Most of us would rather be in a state of balance or homeostasis, that is, "static man."

Skilled Responses: The Structure of Magic[2]

Whereas natural responses tend to interfere with or shut down the chances of having any meaningful conversation in attempting to communicate about differences, skilled responses have the opposite effect. Skilled responses tend to keep the talk chain open. They tend not to invalidate the other person.

Skilled responses provide a structure of magic consisting of active listening and assertive communications, each with its various subsets. And when you want to start the conversation out on the right foot or make a corrective adjustment when your natural responses are getting in the way, they act as a Rosetta Stone[2] or touchstone.

ACTIVE LISTENING: SKILLED RESPONSES

Attending and Acknowledging

To establish any kind of rapport with the speaker you need to demonstrate that you are present and care. You do so by attending to and acknowledging the speaker. You could actually be very much attuned to what the speaker is trying to communicate, but if you do not demonstrate your attentiveness or appear to be preoccupied or apathetic you are not going to engage the speaker.

---

[2] An inscribed stone found near Rosetta (now called Rashid) on the western mouth of the Nile in Egypt in 1799. Its text is written in three scripts: hieroglyphic, demotic, and Greek. The deciphering of the hieroglyphics by Jean-Francois Champollion in 1822 led to the interpretation of many other early records of many other early Egyptian civilizations. (Oxford Dictionary of English)

You demonstrate your presence by making eye contact and utterances such as *"I see"; "Really?"; "Oh?"; "uh-huh"; "okay"; "wow"; and, "yea."* There may be some inflection in your voice but for the most part probably a steady tone.

Inquiry

Inquiry is asking questions and gathering information. When inquiring you are consulting the speaker to better understand or clarify, as necessary and appropriate, the speaker's message, that is, their meaning, feeling, or motive.

> *"The most important thing in communication is to hear what isn't being said."*
>
> —Peter F. Drucker

Your voice or tone is important in asking questions. You want a tone that comes across as inquisitive but not judgmental. You are asking for a reason—to better understand the speaker.

But aren't you interrupting when inquiring? Good question. The key is that if you keep the agenda with the speaker your probe most times will be interrupted as constructive and not interrupting in that you are seeking to understand and not to divert or take over the conversation. When you start putting in your own two cents, such as "Let me tell you about a similar situation I had," and the like, your line of inquiry most likely be perceived as interrupting. This is an important distinction. So, keep the agenda with the speaker.

There are two types of inquiry: closed-ended questions and open-ended questions. You probably are aware of these two types of probes.

Closed inquiries are designed to elicit short definitive responses, often with just a "yes" or "no" reply.

Examples: *"Do you think you're making progress?"*

"How long have you been working for him?"

Closed inquiries are valuable when you want to get a specific question answered or gather some relevant data.

Open inquiries are designed to have the speaker express herself regarding a question you have.

Examples: *"Can you describe for me what that looks like."*

"Could you give me an example of such an instance?"

"How does that occur?"

When inquiring, *avoid the "why?" question*. Why is that? Well even though the word "why" is certainly an inquiry, it often is inferred that you are judging. That you are thinking that the person could have or should have done something different. *"Why did you do that?"*

Paraphrasing/Speculating

Paraphrasing is translating in your own words what you think the speaker's meaning, feeling, or motive, or all three, is. You are checking out your understanding of the message.

For example:

"You're puzzled about what to do next."

"You just want to talk this out."

"You're surprised and shocked about what happened."

Paraphrasing is not repeating back words verbatim like a recorder. Mirroring is not paraphrasing/speculating. What you are trying to do is verify your understanding of the essence of the message briefly in your own words.

Avoid starter phrases such as: *"In other words…;" "I hear you saying that…;" "If I am reading you right…,"* and so forth. Such phrases are not needed. The sender knows what you are trying to do, that is, capture their meaning, feeling, or motive. Not only are starter phrases not necessary, but they are a turn-off when repeated. Get right to your translation.

Avoid being judgmental in voicing your translation.

When *speculating* you are going beyond paraphrasing. You are taking your translation and interpreting what you think the real meaning, feeling or motive is even though it was not distinctly expressed.

Figure 5.5: Distinguishing between Paraphrasing and Speculating

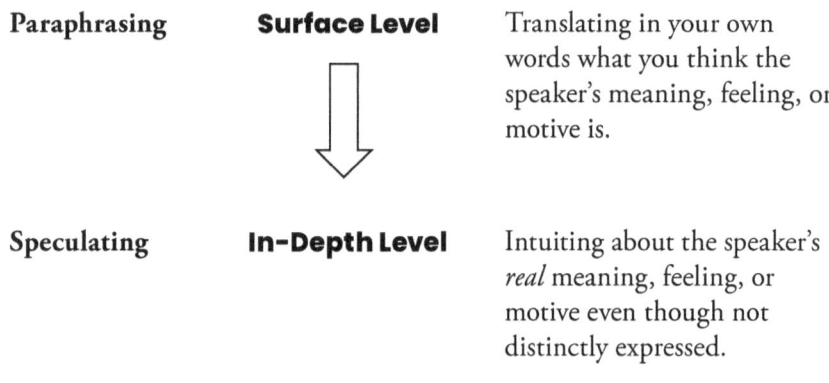

Paraphrasing	**Surface Level**	Translating in your own words what you think the speaker's meaning, feeling, or motive is.
Speculating	**In-Depth Level**	Intuiting about the speaker's *real* meaning, feeling, or motive even though not distinctly expressed.

The following is an example of the difference between a surface-level and in-depth-level translation.

I was coaching a leader who the executive team expressed the desire to welcome to the executive team. We agreed before we met again, that she would visit each of the executive team members to better get to know each of them.

When we met again, she was obviously frustrated as she began to discuss the individual meetings. She started to go into detail about the meetings. I could have begun to probe about the specifics of the meetings to clarify my understanding of what went on. (Paraphrasing at the Surface Level). But I surmised that the details of the meetings were not all that important right now. So, I took a little bit of a risk and speculated (In-Depth Level). *"You feel betrayed?"* Bingo. We then preceded to discuss her thoughts and feelings and the next steps.

Going Around the Talk Chain

Depending on the complexity and length of the message, you may need to go around the talk chain several times before the sender thinks or feels that you have captured the essence of what he was trying to communicate. Each round represents a successive approximation.

A good metaphor can be drawn from my days in the military as part of a mortar squad. The squad consisted of a lead, a forward observer, a gunner, and a loader. The forward observer would use his special binoculars to focus on the target. The binoculars had a horizontal and vertical scale in yards. The forward observer would look through the binoculars at the target. A test round would be fired. Based on where the test round landed in relation to the target, the forward observer would provide feedback to the lead such as *"drop 75 (yards); right 50 (yards)."* The lead would pass the direction on to the gunner who would make the adjustments. It may take several single-round firings until the mortar tube was dialed into the target. When that was the case, the forward observer would feed back *"Fire for effect."* Multiple mortars would be fired in rapid succession until the target was wiped out.

And that is what happens when you take several trips around the talk chain to zero in on the sender's message. But instead of saying "fire for effect," the sender says something like: *"That's right."*

When trying to understand an involved or complex message, you will never get 100 percent of the meaning, feeling, or motive. If you did you would be that person. The person you are attempting to communicate with will determine when you are close enough.

Various Active Listening Roles

In using active listening skilled responses, you may be involved as an interested listener, someone with a different point of view, or an adult friend.

As an *interested listener,* you are attracted to the topic or the speaker, or both.

As *someone with a different point of view,* you want to listen so that you may learn something and perhaps present your thinking.

In voicing a divergent point of view, in addition to using active listening skilled responses, when you speak up you will use assertive communication skilled responses to attempt to have a meaningful discussion or perhaps a dialogue about your real or perceived differences. We will discuss the assertive communication natural responses once we have ended our current discussion regarding the active listening skilled responses.

As an *adult friend* you respect the speaker, so you naturally perk up a bit when he is speaking. In your adult friend role, you can be of great service just by being present for the sender. Sometimes that is all he wants. He just wants to vent. In such cases, you limit yourself to attending and acknowledging. Most times however he wants you to try to understand him and demonstrate that you are trying to do so. In so doing, you may allow him to gain greater perspective, clarity, or insight relative to his issue or concern. And sometimes he may welcome some coaching about what to do. More on that in a moment.

Working through an example

Let us work through an example illustrating skilled active listening responses and working around the talk chain.

The situation: You have a colleague who wants to discuss an important issue that is bothering him. He has told you that you are not personally involved, but that he would appreciate talking about the issue with you.

Your colleague	You
	When you meet you say that you would be happy to help. You ask what role your colleague would want you to play.
Says he would like you to hear him out.	
	You agree. But you wonder if your colleague just wants to vent or wants you to seek to understand what is going on with him regarding the issue. So, you ask.
He says that trying to understand just what is going on would be appreciated and perhaps be quite helpful.	
	You agree.
	You remind yourself that in seeking to understand you will avoid natural responses. Doing such things as judging: *"Do you think you are overreacting?"* Or, advising: *"I wouldn't worry about it."* Or, interrupting by taking the agenda away from your colleague: *"I had a similar situation once, and what I did is…"*
	You need to use skilled responses to seek to understand your colleague's real meaning, feeling, or issue. Of course, you will be attentive. You will inquire when needed to gather relevant information to help your understanding. And you will paraphrase/speculate to check out your understanding and demonstrate your interest in doing so.

Your colleague	You
He describes the problem that has been gnawing at him for some time. It involves a procedure at work that he thinks needs to be modified. He also describes that people who initially backed the change have not come through. He goes into some detail.	
	You say: *"You're stymied."* (paraphrase) *"And you're frustrated and perhaps feel a little betrayed that the support you thought you had has not materialized."* (speculate)
He says that is pretty accurate. He says that he has not given up hope, and thinks there are some people who he could still possibly rely on to make it happen.	
	Having demonstrated your understanding you realize that you have probably already been quite helpful to your colleague, although he may not express it.
	At this point, you think about whether your colleague would be receptive to you expanding your role. Specifically, to go beyond demonstrating understanding and moving into coaching.
	So, you inquire: *"Do you want to discuss possible next steps?"*

We will end the example here. Hopefully, it was useful.

After you get a chance to practice the active listening skills in the exercises below, we will move on to discussing and practicing assertive communication skills.

ACTIVE LISTENING SKILLS: PRACTICE

These practice exercises help you better understand and use skillful active listening responses.

Exercise 5.1: Identifying the Most Useful Response

What to do

Assume that each statement below was made to you early in a conversation in which the speaker was expressing a concern. Do the following:

1. Select the response you think would be the most useful in communicating with the speaker.
2. Compare your answers to those shown in Appendix A, Perception and Communication: "Answers and Comments."

<u>Statements</u>

1. "I cannot stand that new boss of mine. He is such an arrogant know-it-all. Everything that goes wrong he puts on me."

    a. "I guess all of us have a tough time breaking in a new boss."
    b. "Tell me what sort of things have been happening."

2. "I am really fed up with these reports. It looks like everything has to be done yesterday. Why can't we get a little more notice? There is no way to do a good job. What is so tough is that we spend a lot of time getting information that nobody is really going to use."

    a. "You find it hard to keep interested in doing a good job when you feel like you're under pressure to produce stuff that nobody uses."
    b. "You should not feel that way. It is your job. And if something is not right, fix it."

3. "I am running into some real problems with my group since I got promoted. It is hard to figure out how to relate to the people I used to work with, but now work for me."

   a. "How long have you had the new job?"
   b. "So, the relationship with the people you worked with has become strained since you became their boss."

Exercise 5.2: Describe Appropriate Response

What to Do

1. Specifically state what you would say when faced with each of the statements below that would stand a good chance of keeping the talk chain open.
2. Compare your responses to those shown in Appendix A, Perception and Communication: "Questions and Answers."

Statements

1. "I'm sorry I am late for our meeting again. I really tried to be on time, but I have a lot going on at home."

2. You thought you had made your wishes clear. But then you are told the following:

   "I did not know you wanted this done today. You never made that clear I thought we were going to talk about it in detail first."

3. You are about to start a meeting with a small group you have never met before, and you are hit with the following:

   "The last time we had one of these things nothing happened afterward. All the things we agreed on were forgotten. These things are a waste of time."

4. You come home from a hard day at work, and your spouse greets you with:

"What a day I've had. The baby was crying all morning. The washing machine broke down, and I had to do things by hand. Then I went downtown to buy a hat and I had to wait 20 minutes for a bus. I could not find a thing I liked and everybody was so pushy and the store was so crowded. When I got back the babysitter had the stew burnt—and I had worked so hard on it. I am so mad I could cry. And I've got to go downtown again tomorrow."

ASSERTIVE COMMUNICATION

Assertive communication is interacting and expressing yourself directly, positively, confidently, and with respect toward others, thus increasing the chances of being understood. It is being authentic about your thoughts and feelings.

Assertive communication can be contrasted with *aggressive communication* which is a hard-charging approach, often carried out in a hostile manner, where the person comes across as controlling or dominating.

The three assertive communication skilled responses are: Describing; Stating Thoughts; and, Stating Feelings. We will discuss and practice each of these skilled responses in just a bit.

But first, let us discuss the *"I message." The "I message" is the cornerstone of assertive communication.*

The "I" message involves:

- Getting in touch with your observations, thoughts, and feelings regarding WIGO.
- Expressing those observations, thoughts, and feelings authentically.

The opposite of the I message is the *"You message,"* which is the cornerstone of aggressive communication.

Figure 5.6: Contrasting "You messages" and "I messages"

"You message"		"I message"
Judgment or belief regarding what you said or did, or who you are.	**What It Is**	My observation, thoughts, or feelings about what you said, did, or who you are and the impact on me.
Evaluating YOU.	**Focus**	Being authentic about ME. "Touching bases" with my thoughts and feelings.
"You didn't explain it very well."	**Example**	*"I just don't get it."*
Perceived as an attack.	**Likely Result**	Better chance of keeping the talk chain open, allowing any differences to be discussed.

In using the I message you acknowledge ownership of your reaction to WIGO and express yourself accordingly. This ownership of observations, thoughts, and feelings, and the resultant expression (I message) most likely will make the other person less defensive than if you went out to the other person with a You message. The less the other person feels the need to go on the defensive, the more likely the both of you will be able to focus on any divergent viewpoints instead of each other.

The use of the I message does not necessarily mean that you will begin all your statements with "I," although that will generally be the case. For example, a statement such as: "The more we analyze, the more confusing things get for me," represents a genuine statement of frustration without using the word "I."

Conversely, just using "I" does not necessarily make a statement an I message. For example, "I don't think your idea has much merit" most likely will be perceived as an attack, not an I message.

Do not think for a moment that there is anything soft about a skillfully expressed I message. It can be a powerful message. It does not take much skill to "clam up" (sullen silence); lash back (attack); or make a joke (deceiving). In fact, kids are great at such natural responses. But it takes skill and some courage to be authentic about yourself.

A couple of *important guidelines* for you in becoming skillful in using I messages:

- **Be succinct.**

    "Touch bases with yourself" in authentically verbalizing your observations, thoughts, or feelings. Do not go on at length. Nobody wants to listen to a five-minute I message.

- **Go back and forth in a conversation about differences.**

    That is, "touch bases with yourself," and then go back to the other person with an Inquiry. For example: *"What are your thoughts about what I just said?"* Or a Paraphrase/Speculate. For example: *"Based on your earlier comments, I am thinking you may have some reservations about what I just said. Am I correct?"* (Speculate + Inquiry). Pemberton coined such back-and forth-communication flow as "the conversational two-step."

Due to the pivotal role the I message plays in assertive communication, it was advantageous to review the concept here before looking at each of the subset skills. Now let us turn to each of the assertive communication skilled responses.

ASSERTIVE COMMUNICATION: SKILLED RESPONSES

Describing

Describing is stating a topic, someone's earlier statements, or behaviors you want to talk about. When describing, do so in observable and objective terms without interpreting or judging.

Some important thoughts regarding describing:

- Focus on the topic, behavior, or action, not the person.
- Be direct and sincere.
- When a context is needed, start by providing it.

    For example:

    "I'd like to discuss the concern you raised yesterday in the staff meeting about the need to gain greater clarity relative to individual authorities."

    "I noticed this week that in our two project meetings, you did not share any ideas or provide any input."

- If the context is not needed, just go into your I message stating your thought or feeling. For example, *"I do not think we share the same enthusiasm about the boss' proposal. I have some real issues with it."*

- When something happens in the moment you want to respond to, do so. For example, *"I need to stop you right there. I just do not see it that way."* Or, when you want to talk about something, in general, that does not focus on a specific statement or behavior. For example, *"I think we need to talk about our relationship."*

- After describing what you want to talk about, or after stating a thought or feeling, most times it is useful to go back to the other person with a skilled response, that is, an inquiry or paraphrase/speculate. For example, you may have expressed a desire to talk about one of your staff member's waning enthusiasm for a piece of work. You could follow on with an inquiry such, as: *"Am I right?"* Or speculation, such as: *"Is the assignment becoming too routine for you?"*

Stating Thoughts

Stating thoughts is just that. You are expressing your thinking and taking responsibility regarding how a situation, statement, or behavior affects you.

For example:

> *"I find what has happened to be unclear and puzzling."*
>
> *"I think the new procedure is a big improvement."*

Some important thoughts regarding stating thoughts:

- Use "I" messages, or "me" or "my" messages, to indicate that you own the thought.
- Express your thought in positive terms.
- As needed, constructively give reasons to explain the basis for your thoughts.

Stating Feelings

Stating feelings is expressing the emotion you feel about a situation, statement, or behavior.

As with stating thoughts, you are expressing the impact the situation, statement, or behavior has on you. The difference is that you are stating emotions. Thoughts are not emotions.

Some important thoughts regarding stating feelings;

- Describe the feeling you have, positive, negative, or neutral.

    For example:

    "I am annoyed."

    "I am delighted about the progress to date."

- State the feeling in sincere and constructive terms.

    For example:

    "I am angered when you do that." Not: *"I detest you when you do that."*

- Focus on the situation, statement, or behavior, not the person.

- Linking feelings to a description of a specific situation, statement, or behavior that triggered those feelings adds useful context.

    For example:

    "Sam, when we disagree you often use an awful lot of profanity. (Describing) This bothers me (Stating Feelings). In fact, the profanity drowns out for me what you are disturbed about." (Stating Thoughts)

Providing Constructive Feedback

The review of the assertive communication skills of describing, stating thoughts, and stating feelings, along with an understanding of The Ladder of Inference discussed earlier, facilitates recognizing the difference between providing constructive feedback, positive or negative, and criticism or praise—an important distinction.

Constructive Feedback:	Stating *observations* regarding another person's specific behavior or actions and the impact of those behaviors or actions on you.
Praise:	Expressing a *favorable opinion* of what a person said or did, or who they are.
Criticism:	Expressing an *unfavorable opinion* of what another person said or did, or who they are.

Constructive feedback can be used for both positive and negative reinforcement. It works better than praise or criticism in wanting to see desirable behaviors or actions continued or undesirable behaviors or actions diminished or eliminated. The reason is that constructive feedback provides specific and timely information to the receiver rather than generalities.

ASSERTIVE COMMUNICATION SKILLS: PRACTICE

Exercise 5.3: Converting "You Messages" to "I Messages"

What to Do

1. Convert these "You messages" to "I messages." In doing so, as appropriate, describe the situation or behavior and its impact on you by stating a thought or feeling. You are going to have to ad-lib a bit.
2. Compare your responses to those shown in Appendix A, Perception and Communication: "Questions and Answers."

"You messages"

1. "You should stop talking that way."
2. "Your idea won't work."
3. "Why are you always too busy to talk to me when I call?"

Exercise 5.4: The New Safety Procedure

What to Do

1. Read the situation below.
2. Using the structure provided, state what you would say to Pete.
3. Compare what you would say to the response shown in Appendix A: Perception and Communication: "Questions and Answers."

The situation

A new safety procedure was recently implemented with your group. You told your staff about the importance of following this procedure in their work. You have noticed Pete does not use the procedure. In fact, earlier today you heard him say to a co-worker that he will not bother with the new procedure because it will only slow him down. This procedure is a requirement. You need to talk to Pete.

   a. *Describe* what you want to talk to Pete about.
   b. *State your thoughts* and/or *feelings* about the situation.
   c. Reach out to Pete and get him involved in the conversation with an *inquiry* or a *paraphrase/speculate*.

KEEPING THINGS MOVING

Let us now discuss some of the ways you can optimize your conversations, especially your tough conversations. We have already discussed some of these pointers. They are included here as a matter of emphasis and to provide a fuller explanation.

Remember the 3 Rs of Effective Communications

Role: What's my role?

   Am I a player here?

Is this really that important to me? What would happen if I left it alone?

Can I influence the situation?

What's the proper timing, and who should be involved?

Risk: Appreciate that effective communication when dealing with tough conversations is risky. It is risky because you never know what you are going to find as you are authentic about yourself and really trying to understand others.

Responsibility: I will clean up any messes I may have created in seeking to understand or be understood. I will the skillful communication patterns to do so.

Maintain a Growth Mindset

Your objective in communicating about differences should not be to win, convert, change, or even educate someone. You should go into such conversations to seek to understand and to be understood. In such conversations, the hope is that each party gains greater clarity regarding their respective points of view. And perhaps have some learning and growth as well.

A reminder. Referring to the Stages of Awareness discussed earlier in this chapter, the higher the level of awareness of the person you are attempting to communicate with, in general, or concerning a specific topic, the easier it will be to have a respectful and constructive exchange. Dealing with a Stage II person with an absolutistic or fixed mindset is normally tough sledding. This does not mean that you should not try. It is just going to be tougher than trying to communicate with a Stage III, Relativistic, or Stage IV, Transitory, person with a more growth-oriented mindset.

After being frustrated with trying to communicate about a difference with a fixed mindset, again regarding a specific topic or issue, or in general, the best thing is to avoid discussing the subject with that person, or if feasible, avoid the person. It is just not worth your time and effort. That person could be just too toxic for you.

Be Present

We discussed the importance of attending and acknowledging the person you are attempting to communicate with as a precursor for active listening. That is the importance of being present.

And you need to maintain this presence throughout your conversation. You need to focus on the person and her output channels (verbal, voice, and visual) in attempting to understand the real message. In doing so you need to forget about what you are going to say when it becomes your turn. Doing so will only divert you from focusing on the other person and what she is trying to communicate. You will be surprised that when it becomes your turn to talk that you have not missed a beat. In fact, you will be better off in responding because your understanding will be better.

Get a Rhythm Going

You can liken having an effective conversation to dancing. Even though you may not like the music being played. This analogy really holds up when you are engaged in difficult communications.

You want to try and establish a rhythm of going back and forth as you spin around the talk chain. Again, kind of the "conversational two-step." Briefly out to you; then briefly back to me; then back to you; and so forth.

You can create such a rhythm by using skillful communication patterns. Inviting the other person in after your "I" message through inquiry or paraphrase/speculate. And using inquiry and paraphrase/speculate to help clarify and understand what they are saying before you talk.

And this is how you reap the benefits of the Principle of Reciprocity (or Caring) mentioned earlier.

The Principle of Reciprocity (or Caring): *If you think I am trying to understand you, you just may be indebted to try and understand me.*

This principle is huge in trying to understand and be understood. It paves the way for smooth transitioning.

Go to the Balcony

When engaged in strenuous efforts in attempting to communicate about differences, it is sometimes useful to imagine yourself going up to the balcony and peering down on just what is happening. Not to lock in on the words so much, but just to try and get an objective perspective or feel as to what kind of dance is going on.

The 3-Step Conflict Resolution Model

There is the adage that in conflict situations you have two alternatives—fight or flight. Sometimes one of these two alternatives may be appropriate.

But there is a third option. *"Can we just talk about it and see if we can move things to a new and better place?"*

The 3-Step Conflict Resolution Model is an invaluable model for communicating in conflict situations. Thank you, Bill Pemberton.

It is easy to understand, but often not that easy to apply in uptight situations. But using skillful communication patterns in using the model can make good things happen. Sometimes even magic.

Figure 5.7: The 3-Step Conflict Resolution Model

1. Seek to understand and be understood.
2. Seek to resolve ("What's possible?").
3. Agree on the next steps.

Mastering the Effective Communication Patterns Skills

This chapter intends to give you an awareness and appreciation for effective listening and speaking communication patterns to help you constructively communicate about differences. Not only to gain an in-depth awareness but to encourage and enable you to continually hone your active listening and assertive communication skills. To work toward mastering this vital competence. And to use your communications competence in conjunction with a high level of consciousness so you will be a genuine, skillful communicator.

Any acquisition and use of knowledge and skills worth working toward requires dedicated and deliberate practice. As shown below, there are various levels of competence to experience on the road to mastery.

Figure 5.8: Levels of Competence

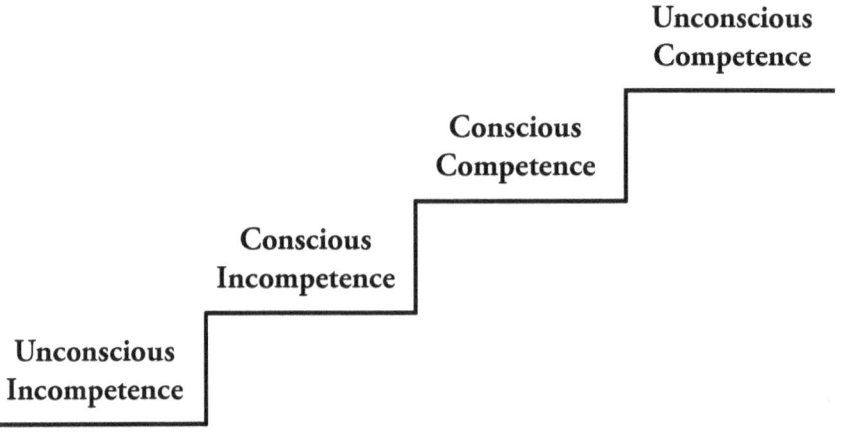

Unconscious Incompetence: I do not even know that I lack the requisite knowledge or skill.

Conscious Incompetence: I realize that I lack the requisite knowledge or skill.

Conscious Competence: I am aware that I have some requisite knowledge or skill but need to keep working to improve.

Unconscious Competence: I have mastered the knowledge or skill. But I must keep my knowledge up to date and my skill honed or they may diminish.

Just as it is important to self-regulate so you can align your communications with WIGO, the same holds true for your behavior. You need to use both your natural and adaptive behaviors to pace with the situation, environment, and relationship to enhance communications and interactions. Using both your natural and adaptive behaviors is the subject of our next chapter.

6

USING NATURAL AND ADAPTIVE BEHAVIORS

"It's been said that we judge ourselves on our intentions and others on their behaviors."

— *What Makes Humans Tick?*
Brandon Parker, Jennifer Larsen, Tony Alessandra

The focus of the first section of this book was to heighten your self-awareness. In this, the second section of the book, the focus is on enhancing three critical interpersonal competencies to help you be a *skillful* self-aware leader. The intent of Chapter Three was to sharpen your perceptive skills in assessing what is going on. The intent of Chapter Four was to enhance your listening and speaking communication patterns to help you effectively communicate about differences. In this chapter, Chapter Five, we discuss the importance of using both natural, modified, and adaptive behaviors in optimizing your effectiveness in important interactions.

Taken together, being a skillful and self-aware leader allows you to operate at a high level of consciousness. That is, to be aware of self and others, and to use such awareness to enhance communications and relationships.

The intent of Chapter Two, *Surfacing the Inner You*, was to give you an understanding and appreciation of your natural tendencies, priorities, and preferences.

As we discussed in Chapter Two, there are two dimensions to your Inner Self—your Core and your Mental Models. Your Core drives your *behavior*. Your *thinking* emanates from your Mental Models.

To review, your Core is the natural or innate you. The elements of the Core are:

- Physical characteristics
- Abilities
- Talents
- Traits
- Temperament

You identified your Core Drivers by reflecting on the primary inputs for doing so—self-observation; constructive feedback; and possibly, behavioral assessments that you may have taken. You then used a one-to-three-word descriptor for each of the core drivers you identified.

Surfacing your Core Drivers is extremely valuable and powerful. Your Core Drivers are your natural behaviors that precipitate your natural tendencies, priorities, and preferences.

Self-Regulating

As discussed in the preceding two chapters, to optimize your effectiveness in communicating in important situations you need to:

- Strive to understand and appreciate the various structures of interpretation, both yours and others, that may be at play in attempting to assess just what is going on (WIGO). One's structure of interpretation determines how the world shows up for him, in general, or how it relates to a specific situation.

- Use effective listening and speaking communication patterns to seek to understand and be understood.

In being perceptive regarding WIGO and using resultant effective communication patterns you *self-regulate* to enhance your effectiveness in having constructive conversations.

The same holds true for your behavior. To optimize your effectiveness, you need to not only use your natural behaviors but, as called for, self-regulate and use modified and adaptive behaviors to best align with the current situation, environment, or relationship.

Most times just being the natural you is just fine. Your natural behaviors can be a real asset. For example, if you have a strong results orientation, taking the lead when a group is spinning its wheels. Or if you have a strong security orientation, stepping forward and influencing the group to gather additional intelligence you think is necessary before making an important decision.

But there are times when you need to modify your natural behaviors or use adaptive behaviors to optimize your interactions.

When involved in important interactions, two instances call for modifying or shifting your natural behaviors. They are:

1. When your natural behavior, which again can be a real asset, can turn into a liability by overdoing it. In such instances, you need to *modify* your natural behavior to not get in the way of effectively interacting. You need to put on the brakes or step on the accelerator to pace with the current situation, environment, or relationship.

2. When you need to *shift* your natural behavior to effectively adapt to the current situation, environment, or relationship.

The DISC Behavioral Style model is an excellent structure to help you understand modifying your behavior or shifting to an adaptive behavior when the situation, environment, or relationship warrants it. We discussed DISC in Chapter Two as a good example of a behavioral assessment instrument.

Below is an overview of the DISC model.

Figure 6.1   The DISC Behavioral Styles

The DISC assessment examines external and easily observable behaviors and measures tendencies using scales of *directness* and *openness*. The measured behaviors are grouped into four categories: **Dominance, Influence, Steadiness, and Conscientiousness**. There is no "best" style. Each style has its unique strengths and opportunities for continuous improvement and growth. In addition to directness and openness differences, there are also *pace* and *priority* differences among the styles.

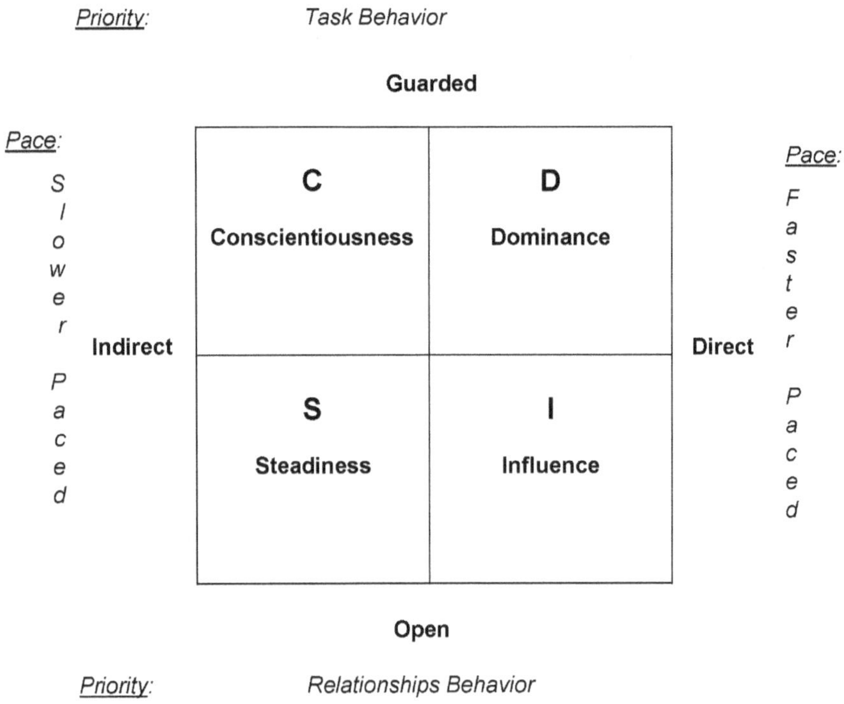

Priority: Task Behavior

Guarded

Pace: Slower Paced

	C Conscientiousness	D Dominance	
Indirect			Direct
	S Steadiness	I Influence	

Pace: Faster Paced

Open

Priority: Relationships Behavior

Modifying Your Natural Behavior

Assume that Steadiness is a core driver and a real asset for a particular leader. It serves him well most times. But when he spends too much time collaborating or perhaps trying to reach a consensus regarding time-urgent issues his team gets anxious as they feel the need to act. In such instances, he needs to be more assertive and less collaborative.

The chart below gives additional examples of modifying natural behavior using the four DISC behavioral styles.[1]

Figure 6.2   Modifying Natural Behaviors

Behavioral Style	Natural Behavior Characteristics	Modified Natural Behavior *(When warranted by the current situation, environment, or relationship, preventing a natural asset from possibly becoming a liability)*
Dominance	**Results Orientation** • Directive • Assertive • Goals • Action • Control • Decisiveness • Risk-taking	• Put the brakes on. • Collaborate more. • Focus more on the process. • Assess understanding. • Test for agreement. • Lighten up.
Influence	**Relationships Orientation** • Outgoing • Friendliness • Seeks approval • Persuasive • Upbeat • Optimistic	• Back off. • Be less impulsive. • Focus more on results and processes. • Follow through on commitments. • Be more realistic.

Steadiness	**Coordination and Cooperation Orientation** • Supportive • Team player • Collaboration • Stability • Routine • Harmony	• Be more assertive. • Be more decisive. • Take some risks. • Be less resistant to change. • Take the lead.
Conscientious	**Security Orientation** • The proven • Completeness • Accuracy • Systematic • Structure • Analytical	• Get to the point. • Accept less than perfection. • Limit expressed analysis to the general rationale for recommendations. • Invite questions to allow for further questions.

For your analysis, substitute the Core Drivers you identified in place of the DISC behavioral styles. Or go ahead and amend your Core Drivers to include or substitute the Disc behavioral styles if you think doing so improves your understanding of your core.

Shifting to Adaptive Behaviors

The focus of modifying natural behaviors is internal. The focus of shifting to adaptive behaviors is external.

Think of using adaptive behaviors as a rubber band. You stretch to pace with the situation, environment, or relationship you are interacting with. Sometimes it may be a small stretch, sometimes much more.

But before continuing with our discussion of using adaptive behaviors, let us address an important issue.

Shifting to adaptive behaviors requires effort and energy. Consequently, you do not want to continually have to use adaptive behaviors. You need to be yourself and only use adaptive behaviors in important interactions, when and as called for.

If your current situation, environment, or relationship constantly requires you to move from your natural behaviors and continually stretch to effectively interact with others, you need to give some serious thought to possibly making some situational changes.

Okay, with that said, let us discuss just what adaptive behavior shifts might look like.

You want to use adaptive behaviors when you have an important interaction, and you believe that using adaptive behaviors will help you pace with whomever you are or will be interacting with.

Again, we will use a chart and the DISC behavioral styles to do so. The chart is shown below.

Your assessment of a person's core drivers or behavioral style is based on your previous experience with that person. Your observation of their natural tendencies, priorities, and preferences.

Figure 6.3 Shifting to Adaptive Behaviors

When Interacting with a Person Whose Behavioral Style Is:	Adaptive Behavior
Dominance D **Results Orientation**<ul><li>Directive</li><li>Assertive</li><li>Goals</li><li>Action</li><li>Control</li><li>Decisiveness</li><li>Risk-taking</li></ul>	<ul><li>Emphasize results.</li><li>Provide data.</li><li>Reinforce the person's accomplishments.</li><li>Be assertive.</li><li>Get on with it.</li></ul>
Influential I **Relationships Orientation**<ul><li>Outgoing</li><li>Friendliness</li><li>Seeks approval</li><li>Persuasive</li><li>Upbeat</li><li>Optimistic</li></ul>	<ul><li>Check-in.</li><li>Be optimistic.</li><li>Emphasized people advantages.</li><li>Use positive talk.</li></ul>
Steadiness S **Coordination and Cooperation orientation**<ul><li>Supportive</li><li>Team player</li><li>Collaboration</li><li>Stability</li><li>Routine</li><li>Harmony</li></ul>	<ul><li>Minimize risk-taking.</li><li>Be relaxing.</li><li>Stress group or team advantages.</li><li>Demonstrate listening.</li><li>Emphasize steady progress.</li></ul>
Conscientiousness C **Security Orientation**<ul><li>The proven</li><li>Completeness</li><li>Accuracy</li><li>Systematic</li><li>Structure</li><li>Analytical</li></ul>	<ul><li>Focus on evidence-based intelligence.</li><li>Stress the research findings.</li><li>Demonstrate reasoning and logical thinking.</li><li>Go slow to go fast.</li></ul>

In shifting to adaptive behaviors, you are not trying to be manipulative. Quite the contrary. Your goal is to align with the person's natural tendencies, priorities, and preferences to enhance the interaction and keep things flowing. In doing so you need to be authentic and sincere.

III

SELF-COACHING: MAKING PERSONAL BEHAVIORAL CHANGES

Leadership starts with you as the leader.

This book intends to provide you with greater clarity, confidence, and competence in being both a self-aware and skilled leader.

We have covered a lot of ground in trying to achieve this intent. Hopefully, you have benefited accordingly. Most likely you have some thoughts about making some personal improvements requiring some behavior change. Thus, it seems timely to discuss in closing a methodology to help you make such shifts.

The final chapter in the book walks you through a comprehensive, practical, and proven process to help you engage in quality thinking and appropriate actions to facilitate making any behavioral changes that require more than a good intention to do so.

7

SELF-COACHING: MAKING PERSONAL BEHAVIORAL CHANGE

Let us begin the final chapter by reinforcing two recommendations made throughout the book. Two recommendations, to not only help you be a successful leader, but an effective human being.

The two recommendations I strongly encourage you to commit to are:

- Have a "growth mindset" as opposed to a "fixed mindset."

    Continuously examine just how the world shows up for you. Be curious. Be conscious regarding your mental models and, as called for, revise your assumptions and beliefs in light of new realities.

- Continuous learning and growth.

    The status quo is not an option. There is so much out there to learn, and to grow in so doing. And to reap the enjoyment.

With that said, let us now walk through a comprehensive, practical, and proven process for you to use on an ongoing basis to make personal behavioral changes that require something more than just the will to do so. The process facilitates you engaging in quality thinking and appropriate actions to make such changes.

Let us lay the foundation for the process with an important principle. I call it the Principle of the Current Me.

Figure 7.1   Principle of the Current Me

Principle of the Current Me: I am a product of:

- the way I think about things (my mental models); and,
- the practices I engage in (my behavior).

If I want to make any personal change, I need to change the way I think about things (my mental models); or/and, the practices I engage in.

This important principle is embedded in the process we are about to walk through.

The Self-Coaching Process

To enhance your understanding of the process, I use a hypothetical example of a leader, Harvey, wanting to make a behavioral change that is important to him.

Let us walk through the nine steps of the process, and bring Harvey along with us.

If you have a current behavioral change you would like to work on you are encouraged to put the process immediately to work for you.

The Steps

1. Goal

"What is the behavioral change I am committed to making?"
Summarize in a well-worded sentence.

Harvey

I am committed to being less directive and more collaborative and delegative in working with my leadership team. They are at a maturity level that makes sense for me to be less directive.

2. Importance

"Why is it important?"
"What would happen if I did nothing?"

Harvey

Based on pushback from my leadership team and my own thinking I think it is time to be more inclusive in interacting with my leadership team as the various situational variables dictate. Such a shift should lead to getting better results and provide a healthier working environment.

3. Previous Attempts

"What, if anything, have I tried?"
"How did that go?"
"What, if anything, have I learned?" and *"How might that be helpful now?"*

Harvey

I have not really made any conscious efforts to shift my leader-manager behavior up until now.

4. **Measures of Success**

   "How will I know success when I see it?"

   "What are the specific pieces of evidence that will tell me that I have achieved the goal?"

   Articulate your measures of success in a series of "when" statements that represent evidence of success.

   ### Harvey

   "When":

   - *Greater staff involvement in problem-solving and decision-making exists.*
   - *Better quality problem-solving and decision-making occurs.*
   - *Easier implementation of decisions occurs.*

5. **Value**

   "What will be the value of achieving the goal?"

   ### Harvey

   - *Staff development.*
   - *Improved communications.*
   - *Improved commitment.*
   - *Free up more discretionary time for me to do higher value-added leadership work.*

6. **Competing Commitments**

   These typically are tendencies, priorities, and preferences stemming from one's core and current mental models.[1]

   ### Harvey

   My competing commitment stems from:

a) *My natural core directive style.*

b) *The mental model I carry around nurtured by previous bosses. That belief is that good leader-managers need to be direct and forceful and to have most of the answers. To behave any differently is a sign of weakness.*

I know that I am going to have to:

a) *Change my assumptions as to what constitutes effective leader-manager behavior.*

b) *Use adaptive as well as natural behaviors in working with my staff.*

I am hoping that the results achieved along the way will facilitate my making these shifts.

7. Competency

"Are there any additional knowledge or skills I need to achieve this behavioral change goal?"

In making behavioral change, most of the time it is not a matter of not possessing the needed competency (the "can-dos"). Rather, it is the commitment to do so (the "will-dos").[1]

Harvey

I have the necessary knowledge and skills to make this change.

I know I can be more collaborative and delegative in working with my staff as opportunities present themselves. It is a matter of me just doing so.

8. Implementation Plan

"Based on my analysis, what is an effective implementation plan?"

"What are my implementation guidelines and steps?"

"In terms of Self-Coaching, "What are the:

- *Specific Deliberate Practices I will follow to help me make this transition.*
- *Related Self-Observation Questions I will ask myself to assess progress?"*

Deliberate Practice: Recurring behavior with a specific standard or concept in mind.

Self-Observation Questions: Questions I will ask myself to gauge progress.[2]

Harvey

Implementation Guidelines and Steps

- *Share goals and rationale with my staff.*
- *Solicit their help in helping me with this transition.*
- *Identify any hopes and concerns they may have.*
- *Only collaborate and delegate when I know that the affected people have the task or responsibility maturity (competence + motivation) to be successful.*
- *Provide coaching when and as necessary.*

Practices

Over the next two months:

Keep a record of the problems solved and decisions made with my staff when I used a more collaborative or delegative leader-manager behavior.

Include:

- *Any hopes or concerns I had when I used a more collaborative or delegative approach.*
- *Any discussion of desired results when doing so.*
- *Any discussion regarding the "Whats" and "Hows" in making and delegations.*
- *Any coaching I did.*

Self-Observation

For each summary I record, select an appropriate follow-up date and place it in a follow-up file.

When each summary comes out of the follow-up file, reflect on:

- *Results of the collaboration or delegation.*
- *Any staff learning or growth.*
- *What I might have done differently.*
- *What I learned.*

9. Measuring Progress

Assessing behavioral change progress is best measured by looking back at what you have achieved to date on your journey, rather than looking forward at how far you have yet to go.[3]

This alternative method for measuring behavioral change is especially valuable for leaders. As leaders, we typically gauge our organizational progress against a desired future state. But this method for measuring progress for behavioral change can be frustrating. So, rather than focusing on the gaps that exist between where you are and achieving your personal ideals, focus on the gains you have made.

Celebrate the gains you have made rather than get frustrated and possibly give up by focusing on the gaps that exist between where you are and achieving your personal ideals.

You can discontinue consciously working on your desired personal behavioral change when you can truthfully say that it is a part of you now. It may not be your true natural behavior, but is an adaptive behavior that you are now comfortable with, and are becoming increasingly skilled in using.

APPENDIX A: PERCEPTION AND COMMUNICATION: ANSWERS AND COMMENTS

Chapter Three

Exercise 3.1: Communication Barriers

Some verbal, voice, and visual barriers that can get in the way of communication are:

- *interrupting*
- *looking away*
- *fidgeting*
- *clamming up*
- *withdrawing*
- *getting defensive*
- *ridiculing*
- *going off on a tangent*
- *monotone*
- *referring to examples or events the other party doesn't share*
- *yelling*
- *attacking*
- *dismissing or making light of what the other party is saying*
- *making light of what is being said*
- *failing to make eye contact*
- *changing the subject before the other party has finished a thought*
- *too loud or low a tone of voice*
- *sarcasm*
- *insulting*
- *invalidating*
- *giving unsolicited advice*
- *being deceptive*
- *busy doing something else*
- *taking or making a phone call*
- *dragging on*
- *using words that the other party does not understand*

Chapter Four

Exercise 4.1: What Do You See?

How about the first image to the left of the page? Do you see a goblet, or is that a fountain? Are twins staring at one another? How do you know they are twins? See none of these images? See something else?

Over to the right, do you see what might be described as a young girl? An old lady? Both? Neither? Something else?

People tend to get particularly irked relative to this image for some reason if they do not see the young girl, the old lady, or both. The point relative to our discussion of perception is that it really doesn't matter. It's in the eye of the beholder.

But here goes, one time only. See if this helps. If not move on.

The young lady is looking over her right shoulder, with a feather in her dark hair. The old lady is looking down, with her chin tucked between what looks to be a fluffy coat or fur of some kind.

What about the final image? Do you see the face of what is commonly recognized as the face of Jesus Christ?

Exercise 4.2: Who Done It?

<u>Answers</u>

1. T
2. T
3. ?
4. T
5. ?
6. ?
7. ?
8. F
9. T

Exercise 4.3: Deletion

There are 6 Fs in the sentence. It is common for people to miss or *delete* the "fs" in the "ofs."

In using this exercise over the years in training sessions I have had answers that ranged from 2 to 8! Must have been the pressure.

Exercise 4.4: Distortion

If you said such things as: "I see a car parked at the curb;" "It is in front of a house with a Mr. Jones attached to it;" "There is a tree in the front yard"; and so forth, you stuck to the observation level.

If, however, in your description you said something like: "Dr. Smith is making a house call on Mr. Jones," you moved from the observation level in the Ladder of Inference and began ascending the rungs of the ladder going from sensing to postulating; from facts to assumptions. You began projecting yourself into the territory. And in so doing, increased the likelihood of *distortion* in your perception of what is going on.

Chapter 5

Exercise 5.1: Identifying the Most Useful Response

<u>Statements</u>

1. "I cannot stand that new boss of mine. He's such an arrogant know-it-all. Everything that goes wrong he puts on me."

    a. "I guess all of us have a tough time breaking in a new boss."
    b. "Tell me what sort of things have been happening."

    The best response is b., which is an inquiry. You asked it because you thought it was relevant to help you understand the speaker's issue. Response a. is a deceiving response making light of the speaker's concern, and thereby invalidating the concern.

2. "I am really fed up with these reports. It looks like everything has to be done yesterday. Why can't we get a little more notice? There is no way to do a good job. What's so tough is that we spend a lot of time getting information that nobody is really going to use."

    a. "You find it hard to keep interested in doing a good job when you feel like you're under pressure to produce stuff that nobody uses."
    b. "You should not feel that way. It is your job. And if something is not right, fix it."

    The best response is a., which incorporates both a paraphrase and speculate. Response b. is a form of attack in that it both judges and advises relative to the speaker's statement.

3. "I'm running into some real problems with my group since I got promoted. It's hard to figure out how to relate to the people I used to work with, but now work for me."

    a. "How long have you had the new job?"
    b. "So, the relationship with the people you worked with has become strained since you became their boss."

    These are both skilled responses and both would be appropriate depending on where you were at in your attempt to understand the speaker. Response a. is an inquiry that you would use to gain additional information which you think might be relevant to you in understanding the speaker's concern. Response b. is a paraphrase of the speaker's concern. You use it because you, unlike response a., think you have a clear enough picture to check out the speaker's meaning.

Exercise 5.2: Describe Appropriate Response

Statements

1. "I am sorry I am late for our meeting again. I really tried to be on time, but I have a lot going on at home.

   Assuming you are somewhat taken aback by the lateness, rather than giving a deceiving response like: "Well that's okay," it would probably be best to start by paraphrasing what was said about the cause of the lateness. Something like: "Lot going on the home front?" If the person wanted to elaborate you might allow a little bit of that, but then move quickly into the plan for the meeting. What you don't want to do is to be drawn into a long discussion regarding what is going on at home. Or, after paraphrasing, depending on how much you are upset, you might voice your concern about the importance of starting on time. (Assertive Communication)

2. You thought you had made your wishes clear. But then you are told the following:

   "I did not know you wanted this done today. You never made that clear I thought we were going to talk about it in detail first."

   What you do not want to get started here is a blame game. A good start would probably be to paraphrase the situation. Something like: "Well it's obvious we had different interpretations about what was to be done and when." If appropriate, you might want to spend a little time to see what you could both learn from the situation and how you could apply such learning in the future.

3. You are about to start a meeting with a small group you have never met before, and you are hit with the following:

   "The last time we had one of these things nothing happened afterward. All the things we agreed on were forgotten. These things are a waste of time."

You might start by acknowledging what was said. A paraphrase something like: "You are obviously upset about the lack of follow-on regarding similar meetings in the past." You then might want to inquire into the group to see to want degree the person's thoughts were shared. Assuming the thoughts are shared, you might want to inquire regarding suggestions for preventing a recurrence and then go from there. Obviously, time will dictate as to how much detail you want or can get into at the moment. You will need to be sincere and commit to any recommendations you think are sound.

4. You come home from a hard day at work, and your spouse greets you with:

   "What a day I've had. The baby was crying all morning. The washing machine broke down, and I had to do things by hand. Then I went downtown to buy a hat and I had to wait 20 minutes for a bus. I could not find a thing I liked and everybody was so pushy and the store was so crowded. When I got back the babysitter had the stew burnt—and I had worked so hard on it. I am so mad I could cry. And I've got to go downtown again tomorrow."

   She probably does not want a string of inquiries regarding further details. And she certainly does not want to know about your hard day. At least not now. How about a slam dunk speculation like: "Wow, what a day from hell you've had!" After she lets you know that you've hit the bullseye with something like: "You can say that again," you can give her a big hug. And perhaps inquire as to whether you can fix her a drink.

Exercise 5.3: Converting "You Messages" to "I Messages"

There is no right answer here because we are not there in the situation and consequently do not know the dynamics. That is why you were encouraged to ad-lib. Anyway, in so doing here are some I message responses that incorporate stating a thought, a feeling, and perhaps a description of the situation or statement.

1. "You" message: *"You should stop talking that way."*

    Possible "I" message: *"I get defensive and lose track of what you are trying to say when you come on so strong. I've been hesitant to bring it up, but thought it was important enough to talk about"*

    (Describing: *"Come on so strong"* + Stating Feelings: *"I get defensive"* (the impact of the behavior) and *"I've been "hesitant to bring it up…"* Stating Feeling.)

2. "You" message: *"Your idea won't work."*

    Possible "I" message: *"I have difficulty seeing how the idea will work."* (Stating Thought)

3. "You" message: *"Why are you always too busy to talk to me when I call?"*

    Possible "I" message: *"Whenever I have called lately you cannot talk to me. And then I do not hear back. This bothers me and impedes my progress on the project."* (Describing Situation + Stating Feeling + Stating Thought regarding impact)

As discussed in the chapter, instead of putting a period at the end of your I message it normally adds to the flow and makes for a more constructive conversation if you go back to the person with an inquiry or a paraphrase/speculate.

For example:

> In the first I message an inquiry is not directly stated, but is implied by the *"I thought it was important enough to talk about."*
>
> A logical inquiry for the second You message would be something like: *"Perhaps if I understood a little more of the rationale behind the idea it wouldn't be an issue for me."* Assuming that is what you really think.
>
> For the third You message, *"Can we discuss?"* would seem to be an appropriate follow-on inquiry.

Exercise 5.4: The New Safety Procedure

<u>**The Situation**</u>

There are no right or wrong statements. But compare and contrast your statements to the statements shown below.

a. **Describe** what you want to talk to Pete about.

   "Pete, I noticed that you are not following the new safety procedure. I also heard that you don't intend to because it will slow you down."

b. **State your thoughts** and/or **feelings** about the situation.

   "I am greatly disturbed about your lack of compliance

c. Reach out to Pete and get him involved in the conversation with an **inquiry** or a **paraphrase/speculate**.

   "What the hell is going on?"

In going back to Pete, a good open-ended inquiry, as shown in c. above, is recommended rather than laying down the law early in the conversation. It is a good practice in such instances to give the person an opportunity to "explain away" the discrepancy. That is, to present their rationale for non-compliance. Again, we are not there, so we do not have a feel for the seriousness of this discrepancy. But safety procedures are put into effect for a reason. After hearing Pete out, you may have some thoughts about making some modifications to the procedure. Or, you may need to give some heavy I messages to Pete stating that his behavior is unacceptable and he needs to be in strict compliance. And, if the violation was serious enough, along with his statements, assuming they are true, and putting that into the context of his record up to now, some form of disciplinary action may be in order.

ENDNOTES

Chapter One

1. James Kouzes and Barry Posner, *The Leadership Challenge: How to Make Extraordinary Things Happen in Organizations*, 6th Edition, Jossey-Bass, 2017.
2. Jim Collins, *Good to Great: Why Some Companies Make the Leap… and, Others Don't*, Harper-Collins Publishing Company, 2001.
3. Brené Brown, *Dare to Lead: Brave Work. Tough Conversations. Whole Hearts.* Random House, 2013.
4. Dr. Wayne W. Dyer, *The Shift: Taking Your Life from Ambition to Meaning*, Hay House, 2010.
5. You can access Assessments 24x7 by going to their website: *assesments24x7.com*
6. Carol S. Dweck, Ph.D., *Mindset: The New Psychology of Success: How We Can Learn to Fulfill Our Potential*, Random House Publishing Group, 2007.

Chapter Two

1. Jerry L. Fletcher, *Patterns of High Performance: Discovering the Ways People Work Best*, Berrett-Koehler Publishers, 1993.
2. Donald Clifton and Marcus Bellingham, *Now, Discover Your Strengths*, The Free Press, 2001.
3. Carl Welte, *Building Commitment: Unleashing the Human Potential at Work*, The Ewings Publishing, 2022.

Chapter Three

1. David Lapakko, *An Urban Legend Proliferates*. Published by Cornerstone: A Collection of Scholarly and Creative Works for Minnesota State University, Mankato, 2007.
2. Ron Crossland, *The Leader's Voice, Second Edition*, (New York, Select Books, Inc., 2008).
3. John Grinder and Richard Bandler, *The Structure of Magic II A Book About Communication and Change*, (Palo Alto, CA: Science and Behavior Books, Inc., 1976).
4. A good book for getting acquainted with the Myers-Briggs assessment model is: David Keirsey and Marilyn Bates, *Please Understand Me: Character & Temperament Types*, (Del Mar, CA: Prometheus Nemesis Books, 1978).

The book not only does a good job of explaining the four diametric types and the many types that are combinations of the four basic types but also has a questionnaire for you to take and identify your type.

A good organizational and publishing resource is CPP: Consulting Psychologists Press, Inc. Palo Alto, California.

Regarding the DISC model and assessments, there are many purveyors. If you are interested in learning more about DISC, my recommendation is to go to www.assessments24x7.com.

Also, if interested, a book by the DISC leadership team is worth checking out: Brandon Parker, Jennifer Larsen, and Tony Alessandra, *What Makes Humans Tick: Exploring the Best Validated Assessments*, indie Books International, 2021.

Chapter Four

1. Alfred Korzybski, *Science and Sanity: An Introduction to Non-Aristotelian Systems and General Semantics*, 4th Edition, (Englewood, NJ, Institute of General Semantics, 1958).
2. J. Samuel Bois, *The Art of Awareness*, (Dubuque, IA, 1966).

3. S.I. Hayakawa, *Language in Thought and Action,* Fifth Edition (Eugene, OR.: Harvest Original Publishing Company, 1991). Previous editions published by Houghton Mifflin Harcourt Publishing Company, Boston MA, 1941.
4. Dr. William H. Pemberton, *Sanity for Survival; A Semantic Approach to Conflict Resolution* (San Francisco, CA: Graphic Guides, Inc., 1991).
5. Gail E. Myers and Michele Tolela Myers, *The Dynamics of Human Communication: A Laboratory Approach,* Sixth Edition, (New York: McGraw-Hill Humanities/Socials Sciences/Languages, 1991).
6. Pemberton, op.cit.
7. Exercise from: "The Uncritical Inference Test," William Henry, International Society of General Semantics, San Francisco, CA.
8. Daniel Goleman, *Emotional Intelligence: Why It Can Matter More than IQ* (New York: Bantam Books, 1995.).
9. Dweck, op.cit.
10. Pemberton, op.cit.
11. Added to model. Thomas A. Harris, MD, *I'm OK-You're OK* (New York: Harper Collins, 2004).
12. Korzbyski, op.cit.

Chapter Five

1. Doc Childre, *Freeze Frame: A Scientifically Proven Technique for Clear Decision Making and Improved Health* (Planetary Publications, 2nd Edition, 1998).
2. Bandler and Grinder entitled their two-volume work for clinicians several years back *The Structure of Magic*. The book covered some of the same material as this book but was much broader in scope. In this book, the term is used in a much more specific way. That is, to refer to skilled talk responses.

    Richard Bandler and John Grinder, *The Structure of Magic: A Book About Language and Therapy,* (Palo Alto, CA: Science and Behavior Books, Inc., 1975.

Richard Bandler and John Grinder, *The Structure of Magic II A Book About Communication and Change,* (Palo Alto, CA: Science and Behavior Books, Inc., 1976).

Chapter Six

1. Assessments 24 x 7, op. cit.

   In addition to their website—assessments24x7.com—you can learn more about Assessments 24 x 7, the DISC instrument, and their other assessment instrument products through the book listed below.

   Brandon Parker, Jenifer Larsen, and Tony Alessandra, with Matthew Dickson Indie Books International, 2021.

Chapter Seven

The first two references listed below were valuable in adding to an already self-coaching process. They each provided an important and unique aspects that otherwise would not be realized.

1. Robert Kegan and Lisa Laskow Lahey, *Immunity to Change: How to Overcome It and Unlock the Potential in Yourself and Your Organization (Leadership for the Common Good)*, Harvard Review Business Press, 2009.

   In addition to identifying the driving forces for wanting to make a personal behavioral change, it is important to identify what personal restraining forces might exist. The authors call such restraining forces competing commitments. These, often subconscious, forces cab be powerful and serve as strong impediments to making a desired transition. It is one's immune system at work trying to protect the status quo.

2. James Flaherty, *Coaching: Evoking Excellence in Others*, 3rd Edition, Routledge, 2010.

   As discussed in the chapter contents, we are all products o the way we think about things (our mental models); and the practices we engage in (our behaviors). I called this The Principle of the

Current Me. Therefore, in making personal behavioral change of any significance one needs to change the way they think about things or change their behaviors, or both.

The author's two step approach of crafting Deliberate Practices, that is, practices with a specific concept or standard in mind, and following it up with resultant self-observation questions to gauge progress is just what is needed in executing important behavioral changes.

3. Dan Sullivan, with Dr. Benjamin Hardy, *The Gap and the Gain: The High Achievers' Guide to Happiness and Confidence*, Hay House Business, 2021.

About the Author

Carl Welte founded Welte Associates in 1993. Welte Associates enables organizational leaders and teams to achieve desired business results by helping them build the organizational capabilities to do so. That is, the requisite strategy, structure, systems, and workforce capability to succeed.

His many years of organizational, management, consulting, coaching, and training experience has equipped him with the requisite wisdom and skills to work with leaders and teams to help them effectively address their organization's opportunities and challenges.

He has held senior-level positions in both large and small organizations. Carl has also held leadership positions in a variety of professional, industrial, and educational associations.

Carl was a visiting faculty member for 12 years at the University of Idaho, teaching in its executive development program. He has also taught leadership and management programs in the University of California's extension learning system for more than 10 years.

His other books include: *Making and Fulfilling Your Dreams as a Leader: A Practical Guide for Formulating and Executing Strategy*, 2nd Edition, Ewings Publishing, 2022; and, *Building Commitment: A Leader's Guide to Unleashing the Human Potential at Work*, Ewings Publishing, 2022.

He has an MBA from the University of California, Berkeley, and a BS degree in business administration from the University of California.

Carl lives in Novato, CA with his wife Dee. They have three children, six grandchildren, and two great grandchildren.

He can be reached at:

> Welte Associates
> 14 Plata Court
> Novato, CA 94947
> Phone: (415) 328-1349
> Email: carl@welte.com
> Website: welte.com

www.ingramcontent.com/pod-product-compliance
Lightning Source LLC
LaVergne TN
LVHW041607070526
838199LV00052B/3018